CONTEMPORARY PREFAB HOUSES

daab

Architects/Designers	Project	

Architects/Designers	Project	

INTRODUCTION

Contemporary prefab design is on the rise, becoming more and more popular every day. Is it any wonder why? Once blasted as a cheap building system that harkened back to the days when homeowners could order a home from the Sears, Roebuck & Co. catalogue, contemporary prefab has blossomed into a viable industry that has created an unmatched enthusiasm for better living standards in today's modern world.

There are several reasons for prefab's popularity. As a building type, prefab promises an affordable alternative to custom home-design. This is significant indeed, since it provides an option for individuals to build homes that are not only within their means, but also customized to the way they live. When one considers that only five percent of Americans can afford to hire an architect, and construction costs in major metropolitan areas such as San Francisco and New York routinely run $400 a square foot, prefab becomes an affordable and elegant solution within today's increasingly expensive housing market.

In addition to enhanced customization, prefab construction also offers an efficiency and sustainability unparalleled in conventional building practices. Built within the factory, prefab construction sidesteps production waste and human and material impact on the job site, making it a greener alternative.

But is there a catch to prefab's promise? Industry experts concur that it is no longer as inexpensive as once touted. However, most architects designing and manufacturing prefab homes would reason that a client's initial investment goes further because, unlike standard site-built homes, prefab houses are simply more durable.

Today, an ever-increasing body of talented architects and designers, including the many practitioners showcased within these pages, such as Oskar Leo Kaufmann and Johannes Kaufmann (FRED), Werner Aisslinger (Loftcube), Charlie Lazor (Flatpak house), Lydia Haack + John Höpfner Architekten and Horden Cherry Lee Architects (micro compact home), are striving to make prefab the next revolution in residential architecture.

Zeitgemäße Fertighäuser sind stark im Kommen und werden von Tag zu Tag beliebter. Ist das ein Wunder? Zu Zeiten, als man ein Haus aus dem Katalog von Sears, Roebuck & Co. bestellen konnte noch als billiges Bausystem verspottet, hat sich die moderne Fertigbauarchitektur zu einer lukrativen Industrie entwickelt, die Menschen für bessere Lebensstandards in der Welt von heute begeistert.

Es gibt mehrere Gründe warum Fertighäuser sich wieder zunehmender Beliebtheit erfreuen. Diese Bauweise verspricht eine erschwingliche Alternative zur kundenspezifischen Hausplanung. Das ist von Bedeutung, weil es die Möglichkeit bietet, auch ohne Reichtum Hauseigentümer eigener "vier Wände" zu werden, die von der Stange und dennoch auf den persönlichen Lebensstil zugeschnitten sind. Wenn man berücksichtigt, dass zum Beispiel nur fünf Prozent der amerikanischen Bevölkerung in der Lage ist, sich einen Architekten zu leisten, und sich die Baukosten in den Ballungsgebieten wie San Francisco und New York standardmäßig auf $ 4.500 pro m² belaufen, ist die Fertigbauweise eine erschwingliche und elegante Lösung für den heutzutage immer kostspieliger werdenden Wohnungsmarkt.

Neben der schnellen und energieschonenden Erstellung und den verbesserten Optionen zur Maßanfertigung sind nahezu alle modularen Systeme auch in einer Art und Weise umweltverträglich, wie man es bei der konventionellen Bauweise bis jetzt nur selten vorfindet. Die industrielle Vorab-Produktion der Bauteile verursacht weniger Abfall und verringert alle mit einer Baustelle zusammenhängenden Umweltbeeinträchtigungen.

Gibt es dennoch einen Haken am Versprechen der Fertigbauweise? Experten sind überzeugt, dass sie bald nicht mehr so preiswert sein wird wie einst angepriesen. Allerdings argumentieren die meisten Architekten, die Fertighäuser planen und bauen, dass sich die Investition eines Bauherrn leichter amortisiert, weil Fertighäuser im Vergleich zu den auf der Baustelle gebauten Standardhäusern in ihrem Wert beständiger sind.

Eine kontinuierlich wachsende Gruppe talentierter Architekten und Designer arbeitet daran, die Fertigbauweise zu revolutionieren. Zu ihnen gehören die zahlreichen, auf diesen Seiten präsentierten Kreativen, wie Oskar Leo Kaufmann und Johannes Kaufmann (FRED), Werner Aisslinger (Loftcube), Charlie Lazor (Flatpak house), Lydia Haack + John Höpfner Architekten und Horden Cherry Lee Architects (micro compact home).

El diseño contemporáneo de casas prefabricadas está en auge. Su popularidad aumenta día tras día. Cabría cuestionarse si supone una sorpresa. Tras irrumpir como una forma económica de construcción que recuerda a los tiempos en los que un cliente podía encargar una casa por catálogo –como los de la estadounidense Sears, Roebuck & Co–, los prefabricados contemporáneos han prosperado hasta convertirse en un negocio viable que ha dado lugar a un afán sin precedentes por mejorar la calidad de vida en el mundo moderno.

Son varias las razones que justifican la actual popularidad de los prefabricados. Consideradas como un tipo de construcción, las casas prefabricadas se presentan como una alternativa asequible para una casa de diseño personalizado. Este extremo es de gran relevancia, puesto que se tiene así la posibilidad de construir casas que no solo estén en consonancia con las posibilidades del cliente, sino que además se adecuen a su estilo de vida. Si se tiene en cuenta que únicamente el 5% de los estadounidenses puede costearse la contratación de un arquitecto, y que los costes de construcción en grandes áreas metropolitanas como San Francisco o Nueva York suelen rondar los $ 4.500 por m², las casas prefabricadas pasan a ser una solución factible y elegante en el cada vez más inasequible mercado inmobiliario actual.

Además de ser posible personalizar cada vez más las construcciones prefabricadas, estas ofrecen una eficiencia y un nivel de sostenibilidad sin paragón en las prácticas de construcción convencionales. Confeccionadas en fabricas, las construcciones prefabricadas reducen el volumen de residuos y el impacto humano y material en la zona de trabajo, convirtiéndose en una alternativa ecológica.

Pero ¿no tienen defectos las casas prefabricadas? Los expertos del sector coinciden en apuntar que ya no son tan económicas. No obstante, muchos arquitectos dedicados al diseño y confección de casas prefabricadas lo justifican argumentando que la inversión inicial del cliente se amortiza a más largo plazo porque, a diferencia de las habituales viviendas de obra, las casas prefabricadas sencillamente resisten más.

Hoy en día, un grupo cada vez más numeroso de arquitectos y diseñadores muy cualificados, entre los que se encuentran muchos de los que se presentan en estas páginas, como Oskar Leo Kaufmann y Johannes Kaufmann (FRED), Werner Aisslinger (Loftcube), Charlie Lazor (Flatpak house), Lydia Haack + John Höpfner Architekten y Horden Cherry Lee Architects (micro compact home), se están esforzando por conseguir que las casas prefabricadas representen la próxima revolución de la arquitectura residencial.

Le préfabriqué contemporain a la côte, et devient de plus en plus apprécié chaque jour. Faut-il se demander pourquoi ? Autrefois catalogué comme un système de construction économique, rappelant les jours où les propriétaires pouvaient commander une maison dans le catalogue de Sears, Roebuck & Co., le préfabriqué contemporain apparaît aujourd'hui comme une industrie viable qui suscite un enthousiasme inégalé pour de nouvelles normes de vie dans le monde d'aujourd'hui.

La popularité du préfabriqué s'explique par plusieurs raisons. En tant que type de construction, le préfabriqué promet une alternative abordable à la conception de maison personnalisée. C'est important en effet, car il offre aux particuliers le choix de construire des maisons non seulement dans leurs moyens, mais aussi personnalisées selon leur mode de vie. Si l'on considère que seulement 5% des américains ont les moyens de s'offrir les services d'un architecte, et que les coûts de construction dans des zones métropolitaines majeures telles que San Francisco ou New York sont habituellement de l'ordre de $ 4 500 le m², le préfabriqué est devenu une solution abordable et esthétique dans un marché du logement de plus en plus cher.

Outre une personnalisation accrue, la construction préfabriquée permet une économie d'énergie et une durabilité incomparables avec les usages du bâtiment conventionnel. Construite en usine, la construction préfabriquée évite la production de déchets et limite les impacts humain et matériel sur le site de travail, ce qui en fait une alternative écologique.

Mais le préfabriqué tient-il toutes ses promesses ? Les experts du secteur s'accordent à dire qu'il n'est plus aussi économique qu'on le vantait auparavant. Cependant, la plupart des architectes dessinant et fabriquant des maisons préfabriquées argumentent que l'investissement initial du client est plus viable parce que les maisons préfabriquées sont tout simplement plus durables que les maisons standard construites sur site.

De nos jours, un nombre toujours croissant d'architectes et de designers talentueux, et notamment les nombreux professionnels exposés dans ces pages, comme Oskar Leo Kaufmann et Johannes Kaufmann (FRED), Werner Aisslinger (Loftcube), Charlie Lazor (Flatpak house), Lydia Haack + John Höpfner Architekten et Horden Cherry Lee Architects (micro compact home), redouble d'efforts pour faire du préfabriqué la nouvelle révolution de l'architecture résidentielle.

La progettazione di case prefabbricate moderne è in crescita e diventa ogni giorno più popolare. È forse una sorpresa? Un tempo criticato come sistema di costruzione a basso costo, che ricorda i tempi in cui si poteva ordinare una casa dal catalogo Sears, Roebuck & Co., il prefabbricato moderno si è recentemente convertito in una industria possibile che ha creato un impegno senza precedenti nella ricerca di un più elevato standard abitativo nel mondo moderno.

Le ragioni della popolarità dei prefabbricati sono numerose. Il sistema prefabbricato promette un'alternativa economicamente accessibile alla casa tradizionale, offrendo inoltre la possibilità di personalizzare il progetto adattandolo al proprio lo stile di vita . Se si considera che solo il cinque percento degli americani si può permettere di avvalersi dei servizi di un architetto e che i costi di costruzione nelle maggiori aree metropolitane come San Francisco e New York si aggirano intorno ai $ 4.500 per m², le case prefabbricate diventano una soluzione economicamente accessibile ed elegante nel sempre più caro mercato immobiliare dei giorni nostri.

In aggiunta all'aumentata personalizzazione, le costruzioni prefabbricate offrono anche un'efficienza e una sostenibilità impareggiabile rispetto alle costruzioni convenzionali. La costruzione in fabbrica permette di ridurre la produzione di rifiuti facilitandone lo smaltimento e riducendo l'impatto umano e materiale sul luogo della messa in posa, creando così un'alternativa ecologica.

Non hanno forse difetti le case prefabbricate? Gli esperti industriali sono d'accordo sul fatto che non sono più così economiche come un tempo propagandato. Tuttavia, gran parte degli architetti che progettano e fabbricano case prefabbricate direbbero che il valore dell'investimento iniziale dei clienti è più facilmente ammortizzabile, perchè, a differenza delle case comuni costruite in loco, le case prefabbricate sono semplicemente più durature.

Oggigiorno, un numero sempre crescente di architetti e designer di talento, inclusi i numerosi professionisti i cui progetti sono pubblicati in queste pagine, come Oskar Leo Kaufmann e Johannes Kaufmann (FRED), Werner Aisslinger (Loftcube), Charlie Lazor (Flatpak house), Lydia Haack + John Höpfner Architekten e Horden Cherry Lee Architects (micro compact home), si impegnano affinché le case prefabbricate diventino la prossima rivoluzione dell'architettura residenziale.

AGPS ARCHITECTURE | ZURICH, SWITZERLAND

Website	www.agps.ch
Project	Haus Trüb
Location	Horgen, Zurich, Switzerland
Building materials	Top house: roof insulated wooden plates supported by 30 prefabricated paneled walls
	Lower house: 7 fabricated concrete beams sitting atop poured concrete walls
Building manufacturer	Blumer Elementtechnik AG
Photos	Reinhard Zimmermann, Gaston Wicky (p. 18)

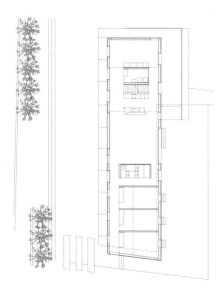

Comprised of two houses, one atop the other, the ground-level house is constructed of wood and its subterranean counterpart is made of concrete. The roof of the wooden house is made from insulated, wooden plates supported by thirty, prefabricated wall panels. The lower building has also utilized prefabricated building systems: it is constructed from seven, fabricated concrete beams sitting atop poured concrete walls.

Bestehend aus zwei übereinander liegenden Häusern, wird das ebenerdig liegende Haus aus Holz konstruiert, während sein unterirdisches Gegenstück aus Beton gebaut wird. Das Dach des Holzhauses besteht aus isolierten Holzplatten, die von dreißig vorgefertigten Dämmplatten gestützt werden. Das untere Gebäude profitiert ebenfalls von vorgefertigten Bausystemen: Es wurde aus sieben fertigen Betonlängsbalken konstruiert, die sich auf gegossenen Betonwänden befinden.

Compuesta por dos viviendas, una sobre otra; la del nivel del suelo está fabricada de madera, mientras que la subterránea es de hormigón. La cubierta la conforman unas planchas aislantes de madera apoyadas en treinta tabiques prefabricados. Para la construcción inferior también se utilizaron elementos prefabricados: siete vigas de hormigón sustentadas sobre tabiques encofrados del mismo material.

Composée de deux maisons l'une sur l'autre : un rez-de-chaussée en bois et une contrepartie souterraine en béton. Le toit de la maison de bois est fait de plaques de bois isolées soutenues par trente panneaux muraux préfabriqués. Le bâtiment inférieur utilise également un système de construction préfabriqué : il est construit à partir de sept poutres en béton au-dessus de murs en béton coulé.

Haus Trüb è una composizione di due case sovrapposte: il piano terra costruito in legno e la sua controparte sotterranea di cemento. Il tetto della casa superiore è costituito da piastre isolanti in legno, supportate da trenta pannelli parete prefabbricati. L'edificio inferiore è anch'esso costruito con sistemi prefabbricati: le pareti in cemento colato sono collocate su sette pilastri di cemento.

STUDIO AISSLINGER, WERNER AISSLINGER | BERLIN, GERMANY

Website	www.aisslinger.de
Project	Loftcube
Location	Berlin, Germany
Building materials	Frame: hot-dip galvanized steel
	Façade: SIPO-timber frame, LSG heat protection glass, sandwich panels RAL 9010
Building manufacturer	Loftcube
Photos	Steffen Jänicke

Architect Werner Aisslinger designed the ultimate modern rooftop apartment with the Loftcube. Conceived as a modern, transparent "flying" cube that is relatively lightweight and easily transportable via crane or helicopter, the Loftcube is based on a basic steel frame system. The materials and colors of the modules are variable and the 11.6 x 11.6 foot formula can be subdivided as desired using wall panels. Designed with a flat-roofed city like Berlin in mind, where the roofs provide an ideal foundation, the Loftcube is meant to accommodate tenants looking for a temporary stay in a rooftop apartment with an unobstructed view. It can also accommodate owners looking to dock it on stations designed specifically for this purpose.

Der Architekt Werner Aisslinger entwarf mit dem Loftcube das ultimative, moderne Hausdach-Appartement. Konzipiert als ein transparenter „schwebender" Würfel, der relativ wenig Gewicht hat und problemlos per Kran oder Helikopter transportiert werden kann, basiert das Loftcube auf einem Stahlrahmensystem. Die Materialien und Farben der Module sind variabel, und die 3,50 x 3,50 m große Konstruktion kann auf Wunsch mit Wandplatten unterteilt werden. Bei der Planung hatte man eine von Flachdächern geprägte Stadt wie Berlin im Hinterkopf, wo die Dächer ein ideales Fundament darstellen. So ist der Loftcube für Bewohner gedacht, die zeitweise in einem Hausdach-Appartement mit einem uneingeschränkten Ausblick residieren möchten. Der Loftcube kann aber auch Besitzer beherbergen, die ihn an Orte „andocken" möchten, die speziell für diesen Zweck vorgesehen wurden.

El arquitecto Werner Aisslinger diseñó lo último en apartamentos en la azotea: el Loftcube. Concebido como un moderno cubo transparente "suspendido", ligero y fácil de transportar con una grúa o un helicóptero, el Loftcube se sustenta en un sencillo armazón de acero. Los materiales y los colores del cubo varían y los 3,50 x 3,50 m se pueden dividir al gusto por medio de tabiques panelables. Ideado para una ciudad con azoteas planas - ofrecen una cimentación magnífica- como es Berlín, el Loftcube está pensado para aquellos que busquen un hogar provisional en un terrado con vistas despejadas. También puede acoplarse en emplazamientos diseñados a tal efecto.

Avec le Loftcube, l'architecte Werner Aisslinger a créé le nec plus ultra de l'appartement de toit moderne. Conçu comme un cube « volant », transparent, relativement léger et facilement transportable par grue ou par hélicoptère, le Loftcube est basé sur un simple système de cadre acier. Les matériaux et les couleurs des modules sont variables et la formule 3,50 x 3,50 m peut être subdivisée à l'envi à l'aide de panneaux muraux. Conçu en pensant à une ville aux toits plats comme Berlin, où les toits constituent des fondations idéales, le Loftcube est idéal pour des locataires voulant séjourner temporairement dans un appartement de toit avec une vue dégagée. Il peut aussi loger des propriétaires souhaitant l'amarrer à des stations spécialement conçues à cet effet.

L'architetto Werner Aisslinger ha disegnato Loftcube, il più recente e moderno appartamento per l'attico. Concepito come un moderno e trasparente cubo "volante", relativamente leggero e facilmente trasportabile con una gru o con un elicottero, il Loftcube è basato su un sistema elementare di ossatura in acciaio. I materiali ed i colori dei moduli sono variabili e la formula di 3,50 x 3,50 m può essere suddivisa secondo richiesta usando dei pannelli parete. Disegnato avendo in mente una città dai tetti a terrazza come Berlino, dove i tetti forniscono le fondamenta ideali, il Loftcube è progettato per ospitare degli inquilini che cercano un alloggio temporaneo in un attico con una vista senza ostacoli. Può anche ospitare proprietari che vogliono ancorarlo a stazioni progettate specificatamente per questo scopo.

ALCHEMY ARCHITECTS | ST. PAUL (MN), USA

Website	www.weehouses.com
Project	Arado weeHouse
Location	Pepin (WI), USA
Building materials	Structure: steel and wood framed "tube"
	Exterior: oxidizing paint over cement fiberboard
Photos	Geoffrey Warner/Alchemy Architects

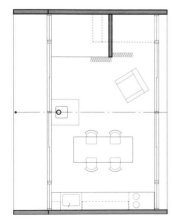

Homeowner budget constraints led the architects to re-evaluate the accessibility of architecture, resulting in the weeHouse prefabrication (module) system, and inspiring a new design platform that can be used for both residential and commercial projects. Only 14 feet wide and 10 feet high the modules were designed with roadway limitations in mind; they can be transported anywhere and combined and customized according to both the landscape needs and the owner's needs. Arado weeHouse was completed in two months for a cost of around $57,000.

Das eingeschränkte Budget von Hausbesitzern hat die Architekten dazu bewogen, die Zugänglichkeit der Architektur neu zu bewerten. Das Ergebnis ist das vorgefertigte weeHouse (Modul) System – eine neue Designplattform, die sowohl für Wohnprojekte als auch für kommerzielle Projekte genutzt werden kann. Die nur 4,30 m breiten und 3 m hohen Module wurden derart konstruiert, dass ihre Maße mit den Fahrbahnbegrenzungen übereinstimmen. Sie können überall hin transportiert werden und entsprechend der Anforderungen des Eigentümers, oder auch passend zur Umgebung, kombiniert und maßgeschneidert werden. Arado weeHouse wurde innerhalb von zwei Monaten zu einem Preis von ca. $ 57.000 fertig gestellt.

Las limitaciones presupuestarias de los propietarios llevaron a los arquitectos a reconsiderar la accesibilidad a la arquitectura. El resultado fue el sistema (modular) prefabricado de weeHouse, una revolucionaria plataforma apta tanto para uso residencial como comercial. De tan solo 4,30 x 3 m, los módulos se diseñaron teniendo en cuenta la calzada. Se pueden transportar a cualquier parte, y combinar y personalizar según el entorno y las necesidades del propietario. La Arado weeHouse se terminó en dos meses y costó poco más de $ 57.000.

Les contraintes budgétaires des propriétaires ont conduit les architectes à réévaluer l'accessibilité de l'architecture, d'où le système de préfabrication (module) weeHouse, et la nouvelle plateforme de design qui peut être utilisée pour des projets aussi bien résidentiels que commerciaux. Mesurant seulement 4,30 m de large pour 3 m de haut, les modules ont été conçus en pensant aux limitations de la route : ils peuvent être transportés n'importe où, combinés et personnalisés selon les nécessités du terrain et les besoins du propriétaire. L'Arado weeHouse a été montée en deux mois pour un coût d'environ $ 57 000.

La ristrettezza del budget dei proprietari di case ha portato gli architetti a rivalutare l'accessibilità dell'architettura. Dalla loro ricerca è risultato il sistema di prefabbricati (moduli) weeHouse e l'ispirazione di una nuova piattaforma di design che può essere usata sia per progetti residenziali sia per quelli commerciali. Larghi solo 4,30 m e alti 3 m i moduli sono stati progettati tenendo in mente le limitazioni delle carreggiate: possono essere trasportati ovunque, combinati e personalizzati secondo le esigenze del paesaggio e del proprietario. L'Arado weeHouse è stata completata in due mesi con un costo di circa $ 57.000.

ALCHEMY ARCHITECTS | ST. PAUL (MN), USA

Website	www.weehouses.com
Project	Marfa weeHouse
Location	Marfa (TX), USA
Building materials	Structure: steel and wood framed "tube"
	Exterior: oxidizing paint over cement fiberboard
	Interior: carbonized bamboo
Photos	courtesy of Alchemy Architects

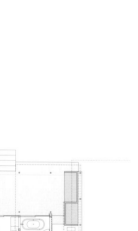

Marfa weeHouse **is the first** of three weeHouse modules that were planned as site-specific. Located at a remote site outside a colony in West Texas, the house serves as a simple retreat. The module is shipped complete with an outdoor shed and a fully finished high-end interior and exterior, leaving only appliances, decks, and sun-shielding canopies to be installed on-site.

Marfa weeHouse ist das erste der drei weeHouse Module, die bauplatzspezifisch geplant wurden. Es befindet sich an einem abgelegenen Ort außerhalb einer Kolonie in West Texas. Das Haus dient einfach dazu, sich zurückzuziehen. Das Modul wird komplett mit einem im Außenbereich befindlichen Schuppen geliefert sowie einer komplett ausgestatteten Innen- und Außeneinrichtung. Lediglich die Geräte, Terrasssen und Sonnenschutzüberdachungen müssen vor Ort installiert werden.

Marfa weeHouse es la primera de las tres weeHouse que se planificaron en función de su entorno. Ubicada en un remoto paraje en el oeste de Texas, la casa hace las veces de simple refugio. El módulo se transportó en una sola pieza junto al cobertizo exterior totalmente acabado, con interiores y exteriores de excelente calidad. Únicamente se instalaron en destino electrodomésticos, pisos y cubiertas solares.

Marfa weeHouse est le premier des trois modules weeHouse prévus spécifiquement pour un site. Située dans un lieu reculé à l'extérieur d'une colonie de l'ouest du Texas, la maison sert de simple retraite. Le module est livré entier avec une remise extérieure, un intérieur et un extérieur haut-de-gamme entièrement finis ; seuls les appareils, les plateformes et les auvents protecteurs contre le soleil sont à installer sur place.

Marfa weeHouse è il primo di tre moduli weeHouse che sono stati progettati per un sito specifico. Posizionata in un luogo remoto esterno ad una colonia in West Texas, la casa serve come semplice ritiro. Il modulo viene trasportato completo con tanto di tettoia esterni, interni ed esterni completamente e altamente rifiniti; solo gli elettrodomestici, i ripiani e le tendine da sole devono essere installate in loco.

ALLMANN SATTLER WAPPNER . ARCHITEKTEN | MUNICH, GERMANY

Website	www.allmannsattlerwappner.de
	www.hausdergegenwart.de
Project	Haus der Gegenwart
Location	Munich, Germany
Building materials	Structure: steel & wood (douglas fir), lined with
	5mm thick galvanized sheet-steel panelling
Photos	courtesy Haus der Gegenwart (p. 45, 50),
	Myrzik und Jarisch Fotografen

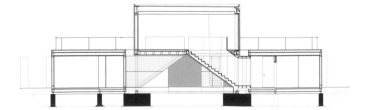

"Haus der Gegenwart" (House of the Present) is the result of an architectural competition in 2001 which dealt with design concepts for an ideal living environment within contemporary trends, and that also considered the question of what a contemporary home might look like for various living styles at a reasonable price. This modern structure built in 2005 was highly attractive, not only for its prize-winning floor plan, with four autonomous living boxes joined by stairways, but also for its electrical systems and home automation.

„Haus der Gegenwart" ist das Ergebnis eines Architekturwettbewerbs im Jahr 2001, bei dem es um Designkonzepte für einen idealen Lebensraum unter Einbeziehung von zeitgemäßen Trends ging. Außerdem wurde die Frage gestellt, wie ein zeitgemäßes, für verschiedene Lebensstile bestimmtes Heim zu einem vernünftigen Preis aussehen könnte. Das 2005 erstellte Modellhaus wurde vielbeachtet; nicht nur wegen der prämierten Architektur mit vier autonomen, durch Treppen miteinander verbundenen „Wohnkästen", sondern auch wegen der zukunftsweisenden Elektronik und der Haustechnik.

"Haus der Gegenwart" (La Casa del Presente) es el resultado de un certamen de arquitectura celebrado en 2001 en el que se pusieron en relación diseños para un entorno habitacional idóneo junto a tendencias actuales; también se tuvo en cuenta cómo tendría que ser la casa actual según diferentes estilos de vida y a un precio razonable. Esta moderna estructura, erigida en 2005, llama mucho la atención no solo por el trazado de su planta -que fue galardonado- con cuatro unidades autónomas, sino también por su sistema eléctrico y la domótica.

"Haus der Gegenwart" (Maison du Présent) est le résultat d'un concours d'architecture de 2001 qui s'intéressait aux concepts de design pour un environnement de vie idéal dans les tendances contemporaines, et qui posait également la question de savoir à quoi devrait ressembler une maison contemporaine pour différents styles de vie, à un prix raisonnable. Cette structure moderne construite en 2005 a été très remarquée, non seulement pour son plan d'étage primé avec ses quatre boxes de vie unis par des escaliers, mais aussi pour son système électrique et sa domotique.

"Haus der Gegenwart" (La Casa del Presente) è il risultato di una competizione di architettura del 2001 che ha trattato i concetti di design per un ambiente di vita ideale all'interno di tendenze contemporanee e che ha anche considerato la questione di come potrebbe essere una casa contemporanea per vari stili di vita ad un prezzo ragionevole. Questa struttura moderna costruita nel 2005 è notevole, non solo per la pianta che, con quattro contenitori abitabili autonomi collegati tramite scale, ha vinto un premio, ma anche per i suoi impianti elettrici e l'automazione domestica.

ANDERSON ANDERSON ARCHITECTURE | SEATTLE (WA), USA

Website	www.andersonanderson.com
Project	Cantiliver House
Location	Granite Falls (WA), USA
Building materials	Prefabricated steel structural frame and structural insulated panel system (SIPS)
Photos	John Clark

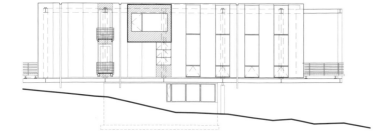

The combination of a challenging topography, geological conditions, and the desire for a high-quality outcome led the architects to a prefabricated solution for many components of the house. The building system is the marriage of two common, standardized, mass-produced building elements: a prefabricated steel structure and a structural insulated panel system (SIPS) that provides non-glazed, building envelope areas. Significant economies were achieved by using the same low-labor, structural panels for walls, floors and roof.

Die Kombination einer faszinierenden Topographie, geologischen Bedingungen und dem Wunsch nach einem Ergebnis von höchster Qualität, brachte die Architekten auf eine vorgefertigte Lösung in Bezug auf viele Komponenten des Hauses. Das Bausystem ist die Vereinigung zweier gewöhnlicher, genormter Bauelemente aus der Massenproduktion: Eine vorgefertigte Stahlkonstruktion und ein bauliches Dämmplattensystem (SIPS), das unverglaste Baugebiete entstehen lässt. Erhebliche Einsparungen werden erzielt, indem die selben arbeitssparenden Bauplatten für Wände, Böden und Dächer verwendet werden.

La combinación de una topografía estimulante, las condiciones geológicas y la búsqueda de un resultado de máxima calidad llevó a los arquitectos a darles una solución prefabricada a muchos elementos de la casa. El sistema de construcción aúna dos elementos comunes, estandarizados y de fabricación en serie: una estructura prefabricada de acero y los paneles aislantes estructurales (SIPS) que generan cerramientos en el edificio sin necesidad de acristalar. Se redujo asimismo la inversión con paneles estructurales en paredes, suelos y tejado.

La combinaison d'une topographie et de conditions géologiques difficiles et du désir d'obtenir un résultat de grande qualité a conduit les architectes à créer une solution préfabriquée pour de nombreux composants de la maison. Le système de construction est l'union de deux éléments de constructions communs, normalisés et produits en masse : une structure d'acier préfabriquée et un système de panneaux isolés structuraux (SIPS) qui fournit une surface d'enveloppe du bâtiment non-lissée. Des économies considérables ont été effectuées en utilisant les mêmes panneaux structuraux, peu exigeants en main-d'œuvre, pour les murs, les sols et le plafond.

La combinazione di una topografia impegnativa, le condizioni geologiche ed il desiderio di un risultato di alta qualità ha portato gli architetti al progetto di una soluzione prefabbricata per molti componenti della casa. Il sistema di costruzione è l'unione di due elementi costruttivi comuni, standardizzati e prodotti in massa: una struttura in acciaio prefabbricata ed un sistema di pannelli strutturali isolanti (SIPS) che fornisce aree costruttive coperte non smaltate. Significanti risparmi sono stati raggiunti grazie all'uso degli stessi pannelli strutturali a bassa manodopera per pareti, pavimenti e tetti.

ANDERSON ANDERSON ARCHITECTURE | SEATTLE (WA), USA

Website	www.andersonanderson.com
Project	Chameleon House
Location	Leelanau County (MI), USA
Building materials	Aluminum frames with galvanized sheet metal cladding, wrapped in a skirting wall of recycled translucent polyethelene slats
Photos	Anthony Vizzari

This unusually slender design by one of the West Coast's pioneers in contemporary prefab construction utilizes industrialized materials similar to those of the agricultural buildings found in the surrounding area of Michigan. The main volume, a tower wrapped in recycled, translucent polyethylene slats that stand two feet away from the galvanized wall surface, serves as both a window-washing platform and an emergency exit for residents. The tower's height allows for views onto a neighboring orchard, while the artfully designed skin mimics the landscape and dutifully changes colors with the passing seasons.

Dieses ungewöhnlich schlanke Design eines der Pioniere der Westküste auf dem Gebiet der zeitgemäßen Fertigbauweise, benutzt industrialisierte Materialien, ähnlich zu den Materialien, die man bei Bauernhäusern in dem Gebiet rund um Michigan findet. Den Hauptteil bildet ein Turm, der, eingewickelt in recycelte, transparente Polyethylenstreifen, die sich 60 cm entfernt von den galvanisierten Wandoberflächen befinden, als Plattform für die Fensterputzer und Notausgang für die Bewohner dient. Die Höhe des Turms gibt den Blick frei auf eine angrenzende Obstplantage, während die kunstvoll gestaltete Verkleidung die Landschaft nachahmt und artig die Farbe wechselt im Einklang mit den wechselnden Jahreszeiten.

Este inusual diseño tan estilizado de una de las primeras edificaciones prefabricadas de la Costa Oeste utiliza materiales industriales similares a los empleados en las construcciones agrícolas en la cercana área de Michigan. El volumen principal, una torre recubierta con listones de polietileno translúcido reciclado a unos 60 cm de la pared galvanizada, hace tanto de plataforma para limpiar las ventanas como de salida de emergencia. La altura de la torre regala unas vistas sobre el huerto colindante, mientras que su ingenioso manto emula el entorno e indefectiblemente cambia de color con el paso de las estaciones.

Ce design étonnamment étroit d'un des pionniers de la Côte Ouest en construction préfabriquée contemporaine utilise des matériaux industriels similaires à ceux des bâtiments agricoles qu'on trouve autour du Michigan. Le volume principal, une tour enveloppée de planchettes de polyéthylène recyclé translucide, à 60 cm de la surface murale galvanisée, sert à la fois de plateforme pour laver les vitres et de sortie de secours pour les résidents. La hauteur de la tour permet aussi d'avoir une vue sur le verger voisin, tandis que le revêtement imite le paysage et change scrupuleusement de couleur selon les saisons.

Questo progetto insolitamente snello, creato da uno dei pionieri nella costruzione di prefabbricati contemporanei della West Coast, utilizza materiali industrializzati simili a quelli degli edifici agricoli trovati nell'area circostante del Michigan. Il volume principale, una torre avvolta in lastre di polietilene riciclato e traslucido che si trova a 60 cm dalla superficie del muro galvanizzato, serve sia come piattaforma per la pulitura delle finestre sia come uscita di emergenza per i residenti. L'altezza della torre offre la vista del frutteto dei vicini, mentre il rivestimento artisticamente disegnato emula il paesaggio e i colori che cambiano con il passare delle stagioni.

BENTHEM CROUWEL ARCHITEKTEN | AMSTERDAM, THE NETHERLANDS

Website	www.benthemcrouwel.nl
Project	House Almere
Location	variable
Building materials	Steel structure covered with sandwich panels
Building manufacturer	Jan Benthem and Mels Crouwel
Photos	Martin Charles

Designed for an "unusual homes" competition that did not take into account current building regulations, this house and its foundations had to be easy to dismantle. The result was a compact house, where the living room is bounded on three sides by glass sheets to bring the surrounding landscape into the house. To combat wind pressure, the space-frame floor structure is attached to a foundation of concrete slabs. Stabilizing fins are placed strategically at the seams of the toughened glass sheets and two steel tension cables secure the lightweight profiled steel roof that is borne aloft by the glazing.

Dieser Entwurf entstammt einem Wettbewerb für „ungewöhnliche Häuser", bei dem man aktuelle Bauvorschriften ignorieren durfte. Das Gebäude und seine Fundamente sollten leicht zu demontieren sein. Das Ergebnis ist ein kompaktes Haus, dessen Wohnzimmer Glasfronten hat, die sich über drei Seiten erstrecken, so dass die Landschaft rundherum sozusagen in das Haus eintritt. Um dem Druck des Windes standzuhalten, wurde das räumliche Tragwerk der Bodenstruktur an ein Fundament aus Betonplatten befestigt. Stabilisierende Lamellen wurden strategisch an den Übergängen der gehärteten Glasfronten platziert, und zwei Stahlspannungskabel sichern das geringe Gewicht des Stahldaches, das hoch oben von der Verglasung getragen wird.

Diseñada para un certamen de "casas insólitas", en el que se obvió la normativa edificadora vigente, la casa y sus cimientos tenían que desmontarse con facilidad. El resultado fue una vivienda compacta con un salón que da a tres mamparas de cristal que incorporan el paisaje dentro de la casa. Para combatir la fuerza del viento, el bastidor que la une al suelo está fijado a los cimientos con planchas de hormigón. Cuenta con alerones estabilizadores situados estratégicamente en las juntas de las mamparas de cristal endurecido y dos cables de acero que afianzan la ligera cubierta de acero nervado sustentado por el acristalamiento.

La maison était conçue pour un concours de "maisons originales", où il fallait présenter une maison sans tenir compte des règlementations en vigueur dans le bâtiment. La maison et ses fondations devaient être facilement démontables. Le résultat : une maison compacte, dont la salle de séjour est entourée sur trois côtés de panneaux de verre pour intégrer le paysage dans la maison. Pour combattre la pression du vent, la structure de couverture du sol est attachée à des dalles de béton. Des ailettes de stabilisation sont placées stratégiquement sur les soudures des feuilles de verre trempé et deux câbles de tension sécurisent le toit léger acier profilé qui repose sur les vitres.

Progettata per una competizione di "case insolite" nella quale non si richiedeva di rispettare le attuali normative edilizie, la casa e le sue fondamenta dovevano essere facili da smantellare. Il risultato è stata una casa compatta, dove il salone è delimitato su tre lati da lastre di vetro per portare il paesaggio circostante dentro la casa. Per combattere la pressione del vento, la struttura con il pavimento reticolato è ancorata alle fondamenta tramite lastre di cemento. Alette stabilizzanti sono piazzate strategicamente sui giunti delle lastre di vetro temprato e due cavi di acciaio assicurano il tetto di acciaio profilato leggero che è supportato in cima dalla vetrata.

BUCKLEY GRAY YEOMAN | LONDON, UK

Website	www.buckleygrayyeoman.com
	www.retreathomes.co.uk
Project	The Retreat
Location	London, UK
Building materials	Frame: softwood stud with ply sheathing and mineral wool insulation
	External cladding: timber boarding
Building manufacturer	Retreat Homes Limited
Photos	Hufton + Crow

This unconventional retreat utilizes a design methodology not typically found in holiday homes. "The Retreat" is a contemporary dwelling, seductive cabin made from timber cladding and floor-to-ceiling windows. It is available in various sizes and is both easy to transport and is flexible, while also offering the comforts of a standard home at the price of 42,400 € to 48,200 €.

Das Design und die verwendeten Materialien entsprechen nicht gerade der Vorstellung eines typischen, kleinen Ferienhauses oder Wohnmobils wieder. „The Retreat" ist eine zeitgemäße, einladende Hütte mit Holzverkleidung und Fenstern, die vom Boden bis zur Decke reichen. Das System ist in verschiedenen Größen lieferbar, leicht zu transportieren und flexibel. Es lockt mit sämtlichen Komforts, die Standardhäuser bieten. Der Preis liegt zwischen 42.400 € bis 48.200 €.

Este refugio poco convencional utiliza una metodología de diseño tipicamente no encontrada en casas vacacionales. "The Retreat" es una vivienda moderna, seductora cabaña revestida de madera y con ventanas que van del suelo al techo. Se oferta en diferentes tamaños y además es fácil de transportar y es flexible, cautiva con el mismo nivel de confort que una casa convencional a unos precios que oscilan entre los 42.400 € y los 48.200 €.

Ce refuge non conventionnel utilise des méthodes de conception qu'on ne retrouve généralement pas dans les maisons de vacances. « The Retreat » est une habitation contemporaine, un chalet séduisant, avec un revêtement en bois et des fenêtres pleine hauteur. Elle est disponible en différentes tailles, à la fois facile à transporter et flexible, et dispose de tout le confort d'une maison standard pour une gamme de prix allant de 42 400 € à 48 200 €.

Il design di questo rifugio non convenzionale è caratterizzato da una metodologia di progettazione non comunemente utilizzata nel design di case di vacanza. "The Retreat" è un chalet moderno e seducente con rivestimenti in legno e finestre a tutta altezza. Disponibile in varie misure, è facile da trasportare, flessibile ed offre gli stessi comfort di una casa tradizionale ad un prezzo che varia dai 42.400 € ai 48.200 €.

DEGER CENGIZ | NEW YORK (NY), USA

Website	www.versadome.com
Project	Versadome Modular Building System
Location	prototype, variable
Building materials	Bamboo composite
Building manufacturer	Versadome
Renderings	D.A.R.E. Design+Architecture

The Versadome is a modular building system whose smooth forms and clean details emulate the organic shapes found in nature as well as the traditional arches and domes found in ancient architecture. Uniquely designed for easy and affordable transportation, assembly and expansion, the building system's energy efficient and low-maintenance structural shells can be stacked and transported in one standard shipping container. True to its name, the Versadome is a compact versatile building system that creates different types of spaces for different types of terrain. Designed for ultimate adaptability and flexibility, the system creates limitless possibilities for a wide range of multi-purpose usages, meeting the needs of anyone in search of lightweight and open plan solutions.

Das Versadome ist ein Baukastensystem, dessen weiche Formen und klare Details die natürlichen Formen der Natur, sowie die traditionellen Bögen und Rundungen, die in der antiken Architektur zu finden sind, nachahmen. Einzigartig entworfen für den leichten und erschwinglichen Transport, Montage und Erweiterung, kann die pflegeleichte Schalenkonstruktion in einem Standard-Versandcontainer gestapelt und transportiert werden. Seinem Namen gerecht werdend, ist der Versadome ein kompaktes, vielseitiges Bausystem, das verschiedene Arten von Räumen für unterschiedliche Arten von Terrain schafft. Entworfen für ultimative Anpassungsfähigkeit und Flexibilität, schafft das System uneingeschränkte Möglichkeiten für eine breite Palette vielfältiger Anwendungen. Es erfüllt die Anforderungen all jener, die leichtgewichtige, offene Planungslösungen suchen.

Versadome es un sistema de construcción modular de suaves formas y pulcros detalles que emulan las formas orgánicas que se encuentran en la naturaleza y en los arcos tradicionales de la antigua arquitectura. Su diseño es excepcional para transportarlo, montarlo y ampliarlo de forma fácil y económica. Los armazones estructurales de este sistema, de gran eficiencia energética y de bajo mantenimiento, se pueden apilar y transportar en un contenedor convencional. Haciendo honor a su nombre, Versadome es un sistema muy versátil que genera diferentes tipos de espacios según los emplazamientos. Su diseño busca la adaptabilidad y la flexibilidad. Sus posibilidades son ilimitadas en un amplísimo espectro de usos, complaciendo a todo aquel que busque una solución liviana y de espacios despejados.

Le Versadome est un système de construction modulaire dont les formes lisses et les détails nets prennent modèle sur les formes organiques de la nature ainsi que sur les arches et dômes traditionnels de l'architecture ancienne. Avec son design unique créé pour un transport, un assemblage et un agrandissement faciles et abordables, les coques structurelles du système de construction, économiques et faciles d'entretien, peuvent être entassées et transportées dans un container de livraison standard. Comme son nom l'indique, le Versadome est un système de construction compact et versatile qui crée différents types d'espaces pour différents types de terrain. Conçu pour une adaptabilité et une flexibilité optimales, le système offre des possibilités illimitées pour une large gamme d'usages polyvalents, afin de répondre aux besoins de quiconque recherche un logement léger et décloisonné.

Il Versadome è un sistema di costruzione modulare le cui dolci forme emulano sia le figure organiche trovate in natura sia i tradizionali archi e palazzi dell'architettura antica. Progettati in modo unico con l'obiettivo di rendere il trasporto, l'assemblaggio e l'espansione facili ed economici, gli involucri strutturali dell'impianto energetico, efficienti e con bassa necessità di manutenzione, possono essere impilati e trasportati in un normale container. Fedele al suo nome, il Versadome è un sistema di costruzione compatto e versatile che crea spazi differenziati per vari tipi di terreni. Progettato per un'adattabilità e flessibilità finale, il sistema crea possibilità illimitate per una vasta gamma di utilizzo con più scopi, che vanno incontro alle esigenze di chiunque cerchi delle soluzioni leggere e a pianta aperta.

LUIGI COLANI | KARLSRUHE, GERMANY

Website	www.colani.de
Project	Hanse-Colani-Rotorhaus
Location	Oberleichtersbach, Germany
Photos	Hanse Haus

This avant-garde design by Luigi Colani and Hanse Haus showcases a rotating system that constitutes the heart and center of the house. The core of the rotating design allows for three functional areas—bedrooms, kitchen and bath—that are united in a revolving system and, according to use, may be entered merely by pressing a button. Functionality, design, and operating efficiency have been meticulously thought out, so that every inch is optimally used. In addition, an entire wall made completely of glass ensures generous light in the single room house.

Dieses avantgardistische Design von Luigi Colani und Hanse Haus präsentiert ein Drehsystem, das Herz und Zentrum des Hauses bildet. Der Kern des Drehdesigns berücksichtigt drei funktionelle Zonen: Schlafzimmer, Küche und Bad, die in ein rotierendes System integriert sind, das je nach Zweck durch einen simplen Knopfdruck betreten werden kann. Funktionalität, Design und Wirtschaftlichkeit sind akribisch durchdacht, so dass jeder Zentimeter optimal genutzt werden kann. Zusätzlich erzeugt eine Glaswand eine großzügige Lichtquelle in dem Einzimmerhaus.

El vanguardista diseño de Luigi Colani y Hanse Haus presenta un sistema rotatorio que constituye el núcleo de la vivienda. El eje de este sistema rotatorio da acceso a tres áreas funcionales –dormitorios, cocina y baño–, unidas por un sistema giratorio al que se puede acceder con la simple pulsación de un botón. Funcionalidad, diseño y eficacia operativa se han meditado de manera meticulosa para aprovechar cada centímetro. Asimismo, toda una pared acristalada garantiza con creces la luminosidad de esta vivienda unipersonal.

Ce design d'avant-garde de Luigi Colani et Hanse Haus expose un système rotatif qui constitue le cœur et le centre de la maison. Le noyau permet l'accès aux trois espaces fonctionnels – chambres, cuisine et bain - unis dans le même système rotatif, et auxquels on peut accéder en pressant simplement un bouton. Fonctionnalité, design et rendement ont été méticuleusement pensés pour que chaque centimètre carré soit utilisé de manière optimale. En outre, un mur entièrement fait de verre garantit une luminosité généreuse dans cette maison d'une seule pièce.

Questo progetto d'avanguardia disegnato da Luigi Colani e Hanse Haus mette in vetrina un sistema rotante che sostituisce il cuore ed il centro della casa. L'anima del progetto permette l'accesso a tre aree funzionali —le camere da letto, la cucina e il bagno—che sono unite da un sistema girevole e, a seconda dell'uso, sono rese accessibili semplicemente premendo un pulsante. Funzionalità, design ed efficienza operativa sono state meticolosamente pensate, così che ogni centimetro è stato ottimizzato al massimo. Inoltre, un'intera parete completamente di vetro assicura una luce generosa nella casa monolocale.

ALAN CONISBEE ASSOCIATES | LONDON, UK
HUDSON ARCHITECTS | LONDON, UK

Website	www.conisbee.co.uk
	www.hudsonarchitects.co.uk
Project	Cedar House
Location	North Elmham, Norfolk, UK
Building materials	Exterior: cloaked in 15,000 untreated cedar shingles
Building manufacturer	Framework Construction Design Management
Photos	Steve Townsend/zzzone imaging and photography

This new cost-effective prototype deploys innovative off-site construction, which simplifies the building process without compromising the architecture of the house. The prefabricated timber panel structure is entirely cloaked in 15,000 untreated cedar shingles, a material that belies the prefabricated system beneath. The cedar reads as a sleek dramatic, protective cloak, which sits harmoniously within its countryside surroundings.

Dieser neue, kostengünstige Prototyp setzt eine innovative Konstruktion ein, die außerhalb der Baustelle gefertigt wird und den Bauprozess vereinfacht, ohne die Architektur des Hauses zu beeinträchtigen. Die vorgefertigte Holzplattenkonstruktion wird komplett mit 15.000 Schuppen aus unbehandeltem Zedernholz verkleidet; ein Material, das über das darunter liegende Fertigbausystem hinwegtäuscht. Das Zedernholz wirkt wie eine glatte, dramatische Schutzhülle, die sich harmonisch in die ländliche Umgebung einfügt.

Este nuevo prototipo de bajo coste despliega infinidad de innovaciones en edificaciones singulares y simplifica el proceso de construcción sin ir en detrimento de la arquitectura. La estructura prefabricada de paneles de madera esta recubierta en su totalidad por 15.000 tablillas de cedro natural, fijando el sistema prefabricado. El cedro es una espectacular cubierta protectora que encaja de forma armoniosa con el paraje campestre.

Ce nouveau prototype économique déploie une construction hors-site innovante qui simplifie le processus de construction sans compromettre l'architecture de la maison. La structure préfabriquée en panneaux de bois est entièrement couverte de 15 000 bardeaux de cèdre non traité, un matériau qui masque la structure préfabriquée au-dessous. Le cèdre joue le rôle de couverture protectrice à la fois élégante et spectaculaire, en harmonie avec la campagne environnante.

Questo nuovo prototipo efficace dal punto di vista dei costi diffonde una costruzione innovativa lontana che esemplifica il processo di costruzione senza compromettere l'architettura della casa. La struttura prefabbricata composta di pannelli di legno è interamente rivestita da 15.000 assi di cedro non trattato, un materiale che nasconde il sistema prefabbricato sottostante. Il cedro appare come un mantello patinato drammatico e protettivo che è situato armonicamente all'interno dell'ambiente di campagna

ALEJANDRO DUMAY CLARO | SANTIAGO, CHILE

Website	www.ftres.cl
	www.espaciominga.cl
Project	casa MINGA
Location	variable
Building manufacturer	Tecno Fast Atco
Photos	Enrique Marin

Designed by Chilean architect, Alejandro Dumay, Casa MINGA was conceived of as an architectural response to the need for immediate living space. It is based on a modular system comprised of a horizontal unit that is exceptionally changeable and adaptable to any terrain. Delivered by truck, the living module is easy to transport and arrives ready to live in. Various elements such as windows, porches and additional rooms, can also be added. The 600 square-foot module and 260 square-foot terrace can be completed in three to four weeks.

Entworfen vom chilenischen Architekten, Alejandro Dumay, ist das Casa MINGA die architektonische Antwort auf die Forderung nach dem unverzüglichen Schaffen von Wohnraum. Es basiert auf einem Baukastensystem, das aus einer waagerechten Einheit besteht, die außerordentlich verwandelbar ist und sich jedem Terrain anpasst. Angeliefert per LKW, ist das Modul leicht zu transportieren und kann sofort nach dem Eintreffen bezogen werden. Verschiedene Elemente wie Fenster, Veranden und zusätzliche Zimmer können hinzugefügt werden. Das 56 m² große Modul und die 24 m² große Terrasse können in drei bis vier Wochen gefertigt werden.

Diseñada por el arquitecto chileno Alejandro Dumay, la Casa MINGA se concibió como respuesta arquitectónica a la necesidad apremiante de espacio habitacional. Se basa en un sistema modular compuesto por una unidad horizontal de configuración extremadamente polivalente y adaptable a cualquier terreno. Se transporta sin dificultad sobre un camión y está lista para entrar a vivir. Se le pueden añadir algunos elementos, tales como ventanas, porche o más dormitorios. Para completar los 56 m² del módulo y los 24 m² de la terraza se requieren de tres a cuatro semanas.

Conçue par l'architecte chilien Alejandro Dumay, la Casa MINGA a été pensée comme une réponse architecturale au besoin d'un espace de vie immédiat. Elle est basée sur un système modulaire comprenant une unité horizontale qui possède des facultés exceptionnelles de changement et d'adaptation à tout type de terrain. Livré par camion, le module est facilement transportable et arrive prêt à habiter. Divers éléments comme des fenêtres, des porches et des pièces supplémentaires peuvent également être ajoutés. Le module de 56 m² et la terrasse de 24 m² peuvent être prêts en trois à quatre semaines.

Progettata dall'architetto cileno, Alejandro Dumay, Casa MINGA è stata concepita come una risposta architettonica alla necessità di uno spazio immediato in cui vivere. E' costituita da un sistema modulare con un'unità orizzontale che è eccezionalmente variabile ed adattabile a qualsiasi terreno. Il modulo abitabile è facile da trasportare ed è consegnato con un camion pronto per essere abitato. Vari elementi come finestre, portici e camere supplementari possono essere aggiunti. Il modulo da 56 m² ed il terrazzo da 24 m² possono essere completati in tre-quattro settimane.

ARCHITEKT ETH/SIA | ZURICH, SWITZERLAND

Website	www.strohhaus.net
Project	Haus aus gepresstem Stroh
Location	Eschenz, Switzerland
Building materials	Structure: straw (Scobalith)
Building manufacturer	Stropoly (straw-plates manufacturer)
	Max Kaufmann in Wallbach (prefab elements)
Photos	Georg Aerni

The prototype, which is coated with translucent corrugated sheets, uses sandwich boards from industrially compressed straw as static structure and an insulating layer. The modular elements allow a high degree of prefabrication. The prefixed corrugated sheets are weather proofed and energy efficient. The completion of the interior, except for the concrete core, is accomplished by the use of straw boards. The raw surfaces of the boards have been partially painted and others are in their natural state. The skeleton is painted from the inside and the sealed floor-plate serves as flooring. The generous windows also function as sliding elements.

Ce prototype recouvert de tôle ondulée translucide utilise des panneaux sandwiches de paille compressée industriellement comme structure statique et une couche isolante. Les éléments modulaires permettent un taux élevé de préfabrication. Les feuilles ondulées préalablement fixées résistent aux intempéries et sont économes en énergie. La finition de l'intérieur, noyau en béton excepté, est faite à base de carton-paille. Une partie des surfaces brutes des panneaux est peinte et les autres restent dans leur état naturel. Le squelette est peint de l'intérieur et les dalles scellées servent de revêtement de sol. Les larges fenêtres servent aussi d'éléments coulissants.

Dieser Prototyp, der von transparentem Wellblech umhüllt wird, nutzt Gipsplatten aus industriell zusammengepresstem Stroh als statische Konstruktion sowie eine isolierende Schicht. Die Baukastenelemente erlauben einen hohen Grad an Vorfertigung. Die vormontierten Wellbleche sind wetterfest und energiesparend. Die Innenausstattung, ausgenommen der Betonkern, wird durch den Einsatz von Strohplatten vollendet. Die rohe Oberfläche der Platten wird teilweise gestrichen, andere Platten bleiben naturbelassen. Der Rohbau wird von innen gestrichen, und die versiegelte Bodenplatte dient als Fußboden. Die großzügigen Fenster fungieren auch als Schiebeelemente.

Il prototipo, che è rivestito con lastre traslucide ondulate, utilizza pannelli sandwich di paglia pressata in modo industriale come struttura statica e uno strato isolante. Gli elementi modulari consentono un alto livello di prefabbricazione. Le lastre ondulate prefissate sono resistenti agli eventi atmosferici ed a risparmio energetico. Il completamento degli interni, eccezion fatta per l'anima in cemento, è ottenuto dall'uso di tavole di paglia. Le superfici ruvide delle tavole sono state in parte dipinte e in parte lasciate allo stato naturale. Lo scheletro è dipinto dall'interno e la piastra del pavimento sigillata serve da pavimento. Le finestre generose ricoprono anche una funzione di elementi scorrevoli.

El prototipo, recubierto con láminas onduladas translúcidas, emplea paneles sándwich de paja comprimida mediante técnicas industriales. Estos paneles conforman la estructura y sirven de capa aislante. Los elementos modulares favorecen la prefabricación. Las láminas onduladas resisten las inclemencias meteorológicas y ahorran energía. El interior, excepto el núcleo de hormigón, es todo de paneles de paja; la superficie más rugosa de algunas de ellas se ha pintado, y otras conservan su estado natural. El esqueleto se ha pintado por dentro y los paneles sellados del suelo hacen de piso. Los generosos ventanales son también elementos deslizantes.

FNP ARCHITEKTEN | STUTTGART, GERMANY

Website	www.fischer-naumann.de
Project	s(ch)austall
Location	Rheinland-Pfalz, Germany
Building materials	Kerto Q Plywood (Finnforest)
Building manufacturer	Timo Schulz e. K.
Photos	Zooey Braun, Stefanie Naumann (p. 114, 115)

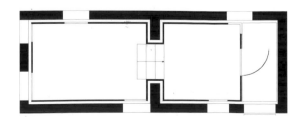

This small building, originally built as a pig stable in 1780, was partly destroyed during World War II, then re-erected and restored over time. A new building was not permitted and a refurbishment was not cost-effective. A house within a house became the design solution, resulting in a prefabricated timber house to independently inhabit the existing stone structure. The warm new interior gives life to the exterior building. The old and the new can be experienced through the gaps formed by the positioning of the new windows trying to meet the original openings.

Dieses kleine Gebäude, ursprünglich 1780 als Schweinestall gebaut, wurde während des 2. Weltkrieges teilweise zerstört, danach wieder aufgebaut und im Laufe der Zeit restauriert. Ein neues Gebäude wurde nicht genehmigt, eine Sanierung wäre nicht gerade kostengünstig gewesen. Ein Haus innerhalb eines Hauses war schließlich die Lösung; ein vorgefertigtes Holzhaus, das unabhängig von der bestehenden Steinkonstruktion beherbergt wird. Die warme, neue Innenausstattung haucht dem äußeren Gebäude Leben ein. Alt und Neu ist gut zu erkennen durch die Lücken, die durch die Positionierung der neuen Fenster entstanden sind, weil man die Fenster bewusst in den Originalöffnungen installiert hat.

Esta pequeña edificación, destinada a cuadra para cerdos en 1780, quedó semiderruída tras la Segunda Guerra Mundial; se volvió a levantar y restaurar en parte. No estaba permitido construir un nuevo edificio y restaurarla no era rentable. La solución fue diseñar una casa dentro de otra: una casa prefabricada de madera que se encastrara de forma independiente en la estructura pétrea. El cálido interior de la nueva casa da vida al exterior. Ambas pueden disfrutarse a través de los vanos de las nuevas ventanas que se emplazan en el lugar de los originales.

Ce petit bâtiment, originellement une porcherie construite en 1780, a été partiellement détruit pendant la Seconde Guerre Mondiale, puis reconstruit et restauré à plusieurs reprises. Il n'était pas possible de construire un nouveau bâtiment et le remettre à neuf aurait coûté trop cher. La solution : une maison dans la maison, un logement de bois préfabriqué pour habiter indépendamment la structure de pierre. Le nouvel intérieur chaleureux donne vie au bâtiment extérieur. L'ancien et le neuf peuvent être ressentis ensemble grâce aux espaces formés par le positionnement des nouvelles fenêtres, qui suit au maximum les ouvertures originales.

Questo piccolo edificio, originariamente costruito come stalla per i maiali nel 1780, è stato in parte distrutto durante la Seconda Guerra Mondiale, poi ricostruito e restaurato nell'arco del tempo. In assenza del permesso di ostruire un nuovo edificio ed essendo una ristrutturazione troppo onerosa, una casa dentro una casa è diventata la soluzione del progetto. Una casa prefabbricata in legno per abitare in modo indipendente nella struttura in sasso. L'interno nuovo e caldo dà vita all'edificio esterno. Il vecchio e il nuovo possono essere vissuti attraverso le fessure create con il posizionamento delle nuove finestre che sono collocate in corripsondenza delle aperture originali.

FOBA (F.O.B ARCHITECTS + F.O.B ASSOCITATION) | KYOTO, JAPAN
TAMAKI ARCHITECTURAL ATELIER | KYOTO, JAPAN

Website	www.fob-web.co.jp
	www.wao.or.jp
Project	S House
Location	Kyoto, Japan
Building materials	Reinforced concrete and steel frame
Building manufacturer	Tsukasa Factory Inc.
Photos	Kei Sugino

Located in the mountainside of Kyoto, Japan, this prefab dwelling is the modern equivalent of a traditional Japanese home. The first floor is devoted to gathering, while the skylight towers on the sloped roof let in natural light that creates a multitude of patterning during the day and later act as light poles in the evening. The interior can be configured into numerous spatial arrangements using either horizontal or vertical partitions. Depending on the season, the main interior corridor reflects the surrounding environment: in the summer it is full of light and warm breezes; in the winter it serves as artful protection from the elements.

Am Berghang von Kyoto in Japan gelegen, ist dieses Fertighaus das moderne Pendant zu einem traditionellen japanischen Heim. Das Erdgeschoss ist zum Verweilen bestimmt, während die Türme mit den Dachfenstern auf dem abgeschrägten Dach Tageslicht hereinlassen, das eine Vielzahl von Lichtmustern und Effekten während des Tages schafft, während es später am Abend Lichtpole erzeugt. Die Innenausstattung kann in zahlreiche räumliche Arrangements konfiguriert werden, indem entweder horizontale oder vertikale Unterteilungen vorgenommen werden. Je nach Jahreszeit spiegelt der Hauptflur im Innern des Hauses die Umgebung wieder: Im Sommer ist er lichtdurchflutet, und es weht ein laues Lüftchen; im Winter dient er als kunstvoller Schutz vor den Naturgewalten.

Ubicada en las faldas montañosas de Kioto en Japón, esta vivienda prefabricada es el equivalente moderno a la tradicional casa japonesa. La primera planta está destinada a reuniones, mientras que la torre sobre el tejado en pendiente deja pasar la luz natural, generando multitud de formas durante el día y actuando como polo luminoso de noche. El espacio interior permite múltiples configuraciones mediante divisiones horizontales o verticales. Dependiendo de la estación del año, el pasillo central refleja el entorno: en verano está lleno de luz y de cálidas brisas; en invierno sirve de ingeniosa protección frente a los elementos.

Situé sur le versant d'une montagne à Kyoto, au Japon, ce logement préfabriqué est l'équivalent moderne de la maison japonaise traditionnelle. Le rez-de-chaussée est dédié au rassemblement, tandis que les tours lucarnes sur le toit pentu laissent entrer une lumière naturelle qui crée une multitude de motifs pendant la journée, et agissent comme des pôles lumineux le soir. L'intérieur peut être configuré selon de nombreux arrangements spatiaux en utilisant des partitions horizontales ou verticales. Le couloir intérieur principal reflète l'environnement selon les saisons : pendant l'été il est plein de lumière et de brises tièdes, l'hiver, c'est une protection astucieuse contre les éléments.

Situata nelle zone montagnose di Kyoto, in Giappone, questa abitazione prefabbricata è l'equivalente moderno della casa giapponese tradizionale. Il primo piano è dedicato alla raccolta, mentre le torri a lucernario sul tetto inclinato fanno entrare la luce naturale che crea una moltitudine di disegni nell'arco del giorno, e più tardi, verso sera, agiscono come poli luminosi. L'interno può essere configurato in numerosi arrangiamenti di spazio usando sia le ripartizioni orizzontali sia quelle verticali. A seconda della stagione, il corridoio interno principale riflette l'ambiente circostante: nell'estate è pieno di luce e caldi brezze; in inverno serve come astuta protezione dagli elementi naturali.

GRACIA STUDIO/JORGE GRACIA | SAN DIEGO (CA), USA

Website	www.graciastudio.com
Project	Casa Becerril
Location	Tijuana, B.C., Mexico
Building materials	Steel frame covered with acrylic panels and fiber cement
	Retaining walls: exposed concrete
Building manufacturer	gracia studio S. de R.L. de C.V.
Photos	Michelle Galindo

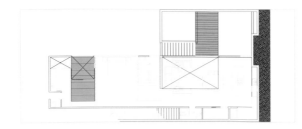

Casa Becerril, an outgrowth of Casa GA, utilizes a prefabricated steel and galvanized metal structure for flexibility, portability and "compact spaciousness." Its exterior, clad with wood, acrylic and fiber cement panels, speaks to the poetic quality of the interior. An open-air patio on the second level, offers expansive city views just beyond the concrete wall that punches the interior to house the staircase.

Casa Becerril, ein Abzweig der Casa GA, nutzt eine Fertigkonstruktion aus Stahl und verzinktem Metall, um Flexibilität, Tragbarkeit und „kompakte Geräumigkeit" zu erzeugen. Die Fassade, verkleidet mit Holz und Platten aus Acryl- und Zementfasererzeugnis, kommuniziert mit der poetischen Beschaffenheit der Innenausstattung. Ein Open-Air-Patio auf der zweiten Ebene bietet einen hervorragenden Ausblick auf die Stadt, direkt hinter der Betonwand, die das Haus innen durchbricht, um das Treppenhaus zu beherbergen.

La Casa Becerril, una extensión de la Casa GA, emplea una estructura de acero y metal galvanizado para conseguir flexibilidad, portabilidad y "espacio compacto". Su exterior, revestido de madera, placas acrílicas y de fibra de cemento, deja entrever la gran calidad del interior. Un patio abierto en el segundo nivel, ofrece unas imponentes vistas a la ciudad más allá del hormigón que penetra en el interior para alojar la escalera.

Casa Becerril, une excroissance de Casa GA, utilise de l'acier préfabriqué et une structure en métal galvanisé pour la flexibilité, le transport et un « espace compact ». Son extérieur, vêtu de bois, d'acrylique et de panneaux en fibrociment, reflète la qualité poétique de l'intérieur. Un patio à ciel ouvert au second niveau offre une vue imprenable sur la ville juste derrière le mur en béton qui perce l'intérieur pour loger l'escalier.

Casa Becerril, uno sviluppo della Casa GA, utilizza acciaio prefabbricato ed una struttura metallica galvanizzata per flessibilità, portabilità ed "ampiezza di spazio compatto." Il suo esterno, rivestito con pannelli di legno, acrilico e fibra di cemento, parla alla qualità poetica degli interni. Un patio all'area aperta sul secondo livello e sul retro offre una visuale estesa della città, subito dietro al muro in cemento che rompe l'interno per ospitare le scale.

GRACIA STUDIO/JORGE GRACIA | SAN DIEGO (CA), USA

Website	www.graciastudio.com
Project	Casa GA
Location	Tijuana, B.C., Mexico
Building materials	Structure: steel with metal stud and wood
	Façade: clad in redwood siding, translucent white polycarbonate panels and galvanized metal
Building manufacturer	gracia studio S. de R.L. de C.V.
Photos	Eduardo de Regules, Pablo Mason (p. 131, 132 top right)

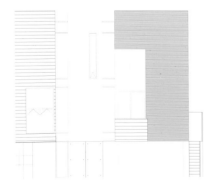

The first prefabricated house conceived and built by Studio Gracia, Casa GA's two structures are intricately bound together by a galvanized, metal-skin stairwell with four glass bridges. The structures are clad with different materials: one in redwood siding and the other in translucent, white, polycarbonate panels. The exterior skin provides a warm glow that adds charm to Tijuana's densely-packed rolling hillsides.

Das erste von Studio Gracia geplante und gebaute Fertighaus, das Casa GA, besteht aus zwei Konstruktionen, die durch einen blechbeschichteten Treppenschacht mit vier Glasbrücken kompliziert miteinander verbunden sind. Die Konstruktionen werden mit verschiedenen Materialien verkleidet: Die eine hat eine Verkleidung aus rotem Holz, die Verkleidung der anderen Konstruktion besticht durch durchscheinende, weiße Platten aus Polycarbonat. Die Außenverkleidung erzeugt einen warmen Schimmer, der den dicht gedrängten, hügeligen Hängen von Tijuana zusätzlichen Charme verleiht.

Fue la primera casa prefabricada concebida y erigida por el Studio Gracia. Sus dos estructuras están unidas por una caja de escalera cubierta con metal galvanizado con cuatro puentes de cristal. Las estructuras están recubiertas de diferentes materiales: una con los laterales de secoya y la otra con paneles blancos de policarbonato translúcido. La cubierta exterior genera un brillo cálido y le da encanto a las colinas de Tijuana, densamente construidas.

Première maison préfabriquée conçue et construite par le Studio Gracia, la Casa GA possède deux structures intimement liées par une cage d'escalier couverte de métal galvanisé avec quatre ponts de verre. Les structures sont revêtues de différents matériaux : l'une d'un bardage de séquoia et l'autre de panneaux de polycarbonate blancs et translucides. Le revêtement extérieur a un éclat chaleureux qui ajoute du charme aux collines surpeuplées de Tijuana.

La prima casa prefabbricata concepita e costruita dallo Studio Gracia. Le due strutture della Casa GA sono intrecciate l'una all'altra tramite un pozzo scale galvanizzato, rivestito in metallo con quattro ponti di vetro. Le strutture sono rivestite con vari materiali: una con un rivestimento in legno di sequoia e l'altra, bianca, con pannelli traslucidi di policarbonato. Il rivestimento esterno fornisce un bagliore caldo che aggiunge fascino alle colline ondulate e densamente affollate di Tijuana.

MAXIMILIANO

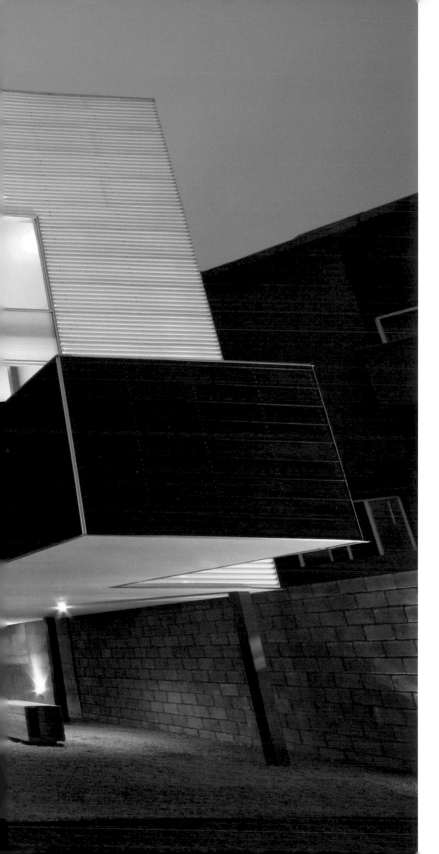

GRACIA STUDIO/JORGE GRACIA | SAN DIEGO (CA), USA

Website	www.graciastudio.com
Project	GS Doctores
Location	Tijuana, B.C., Mexico
Building materials	Translucent corrugated polycarbonate panels and rusted steel
Building manufacturer	gracia studio S. de R.L. de C.V.
Photos	Michelle Galindo

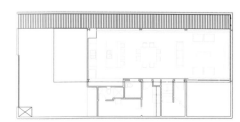

The client's passion for architecture and a desire to live in a friendly, minimalistic house—one suggesting a modern lifestyle where public and private spaces merge—became the first design factors. The building system was uniquely designed for easy and affordable assembly. The exterior was covered with rusted metal and translucent, corrugated, silver, polycarbonate sheets, allowing light to enter and create a sense of glowing in the upper volume over the rigid metal volume of the lower level. The house offers an open floor plan for all common and private areas.

Architektur ist die Passion des Bauherrn; hinzu kam der Wunsch in einem freundlichen, minimalistischen Haus zu leben, was zu der Idee eines modernen Lebensstils führte, wo gewerbliche und private Räume miteinander verschmelzen – die Grundvoraussetzung für diese Planung. Das Bausystem wurde speziell für eine leichte und erschwingliche Montage entworfen. Die Fassade wurde mit rostigem Metall und durchscheinenden, gewellten, silberfarbigen Polycarbonatplatten verkleidet, die Licht hereinlassen und eine Art Schimmer im oberen Bereich über der robusten Metallausstattung der unteren Ebene erzeugen. Das Haus bietet für sämtliche allgemeine und private Bereiche eine offene Raumaufteilung.

La pasión del cliente por la arquitectura y el deseo de vivir en una casa acogedora y minimalista, que evoque un estilo de vida moderno en el que se fundan los espacios públicos y privados, fue el factor determinante en su diseño. Se proyectó un exclusivo sistema de construcción para un ensamblado fácil y económico. El exterior se recubrió con metal aherrumbrado y placas onduladas de policarbonato plateado translúcido que dejan pasar la luz y que le dan cierto brillo al volumen superior sobre la rigidez del inferior. La casa ofrece un plano de planta abierta para las zonas comunes y privadas.

La passion du client pour l'architecture et le désir de vivre dans une maison conviviale et minimaliste – suggérant un style de vie moderne où les espaces privés et publics fusionnent – étaient les premiers facteurs du design. Le système de construction a été conçu de manière unique pour un assemblage facile et abordable. L'extérieur est couvert de métal rouillé et de feuilles de polycarbonate ondulé argenté et translucide, permettant à la lumière d'entrer et de créer une sensation de rayonnement dans le volume supérieur, au-dessus du volume de métal rigide du niveau inférieur. La maison offre un plan d'étage ouvert pour toutes les parties privées et communes.

La passione del cliente per l'architettura ed il desiderio di vivere in una casa amichevole e minimalista che suggerisce uno stile di vita moderno dove gli spazi pubblici e privati si uniscono, sono diventati i criteri principali di progettazione. Il sistema di costruzione è stato progettato con l'obiettivo di ottenere un assemblaggio facile ed economico. L'esterno è stato coperto con metallo arrugginito e lastre di policarbonato traslucide, ondulate, argentate, che permettono alla luce di entrare e creare un senso di bagliore nell'ambiente superiore situato sopra la parte in metallo rigido del livello inferiore. La casa offre una pianta aperta per tutte le aree comuni e private.

LYDIA HAACK + JOHN HÖPFNER ARCHITEKTEN | MUNICH, GERMANY
HORDEN CHERRY LEE ARCHITECTS | LONDON, UK

Website	www.haackhoepfner.de
	www.hcla.co.uk
	www.microcompacthome.com
Project	micro compact home
Location	Munich, Germany
Building materials	Structure: timber frame
	Façade: anodized aluminium, insulated with polyurethane
	and fitted with aluminium frame double glazed windows
Building manufacturer	m-ch micro compact home production
Photos	Sascha Kletsch, Dennis Gilbert (p. 143)

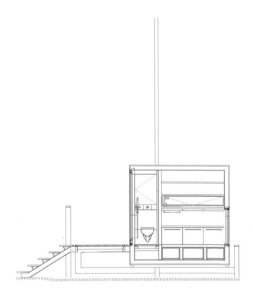

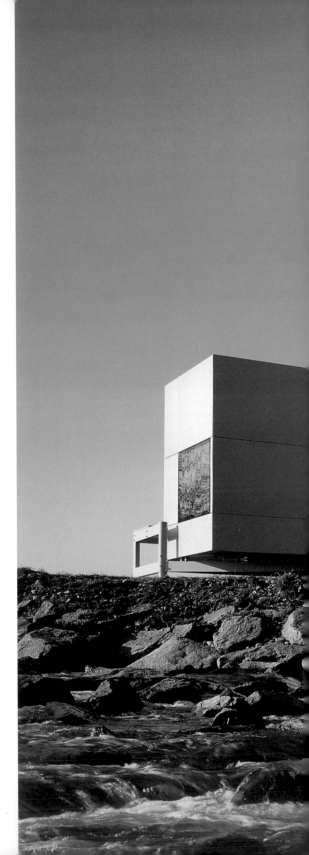

The micro compact home (m-ch) is a revolutionary lightweight dwelling that combines high-tech sophistication with low energy use in a single space-saving, aluminum cube. Featuring integrated furniture and sound systems, as well as a substantially reduced building volume and a low maintenance construction system, it advocates 'less material, more nature,' and is ideal for beautiful natural settings. The dwellings can be easily transported and erected on any terrain without foundations, and offer owners the privilege of living on the edge in extreme conditions without forgoing modern conveniences. The kit includes a lockable external drawer for skis and snowboards and comes with the option of a clip-on, burning stove, as well as log storage for warmth, both of which create the atmosphere of a log cabin.

Das micro compact home (m-ch) ist eine revolutionäre, leichtgewichtige Behausung, die Hightech-Raffinesse mit niedrigem Energieverbrauch in einem individuellen, Platz sparenden Aluminiumkubus kombiniert. Das Haus setzt integrierte Möbel und Soundsysteme in Szene und zeichnet sich aus durch ein erheblich reduziertes Bauvolumen und ein wartungsarmes Bausystem. Es steht für „weniger Material, dafür mehr Natur" und eignet sich hervorragend für wunderschöne, natürliche Szenarien. Die Häuser können leicht transportiert und auf jedem beliebigen Gelände ohne Fundament errichtet werden. So genießt der Eigentümer das Privileg, unter extremen Bedingungen abgelegen leben zu können, jedoch ohne auf moderne Annehmlichkeiten verzichten zu müssen. Die Ausstattung enthält eine abschließbare, außen befindliche Schublade für Skis und Snowboards und wird mit der Option auf einen nachrüstbaren Heizofen sowie eine Holzscheitlagerung für behagliche Wärme geliefert. Beides schafft die Atmosphäre einer Blockhütte.

La micro compact home (m-ch) es un revolucionario hogar muy ligero que combina sofisticación tecnológica con bajo consumo energético en un cubo individual de aluminio que aprovecha todo el espacio. Cuenta con mobiliario y equipo de sonido integrados. El volumen del edificio es muy reducido, al igual que su mantenimiento. Su lema es: "menos materiales y más naturaleza" y es perfecta para emplazarla en hermosos parajes naturales. Se transporta con facilidad y se puede asentar en cualquier terreno sin cimiento alguno. Sus propietarios podrán vivir de forma exclusiva sin tener que renunciar a las comodidades modernas. El kit incluye un armario exterior con cerradura para esquíes y tablas de snowboard y viene con la opción de horno portátil y espacio para leña, lo que le dará un aire de cabaña de madera.

La micro compact home (m-ch) est un logement léger révolutionnaire qui combine sophistication high-tech et économie d'énergie dans un simple cube compact en aluminium. Comprenant des meubles et une sonorisation intégrés, ainsi qu'un volume d'habitation significativement réduit et un système de construction demandant peu d'entretien, il prône le « moins de matériau, plus de nature », et est idéal pour de magnifiques cadres naturels. Les logements peuvent être facilement transportés et montés sur n'importe quel terrain sans fondations, et offrent aux propriétaires le privilège de vivre dans des conditions extrêmes avec tout le confort moderne. Le kit comprend un rangement extérieur verrouillé pour les skis et les snowboards, avec une cuisinière à fixer en option, ainsi qu'un abri pour le bois de chauffage, éléments recréant l'atmosphère d'une cabane en bois.

La micro compact home (m-ch) è un'abitazione rivoluzionaria e leggera che combina la sofisticatezza del high-tech con un utilizzo a basso consumo energetico in un singolo cubo salvaspazio in alluminio. Secondo il principio 'meno materiale, più natura,' questo progetto è caratterizzato da arredamento ed impianti acustici integrati, un volume sostanzialmente ridotto ed un sistema di costruzione che richiede poca manutenzione, ed è inoltre ideale per ambientazioni naturali stupende. Le abitazioni possono essere facilmente trasportate e costruite su un qualsiasi terreno senza fondamenta ed offrono ai proprietari il privilegio di abitare al limite di condizioni estreme senza rinunciare alle comodità moderne. Il pacchetto include un cassetto esterno con serratura per sci e snowboard e viene consegnato con l'opzione di una stufa a clip, ed uno stoccaggio di tronchi per il calore, che creano l'atmosfera di una casetta di legno.

can jump

O$_2$

ugh

HEIKKINEN-KOMONEN ARCHITECTS | HELSINKI, FINLAND

Website	www.heikkinen-komonen.fi
Project	'Touch' House
Location	Tuusula, Finland
Building manufacturer	Kannustalo
Photos	Jussi Tiainen, Markku Alatalo (p. 154, 155 left)

First exhibited in 2000 at a housing fair in Finland, the Touch House is a 2,000 square foot prefab home designed to accommodate a family of four. While the exterior design is not flexible, the interior can accommodate a variety of room sizes, based on a partitioning system and the height of the rooms. The roof is made of glass shingles that create a veranda, a gallery off the main bedroom and a sauna terrace. The center of the home is a double height volume that contains a living room, dining room and kitchen.

Zuerst ausgestellt im Jahre 2000 auf einer Häusermesse in Finnland, ist das Touch House ein 186 m² großes Fertighaus, das für eine vierköpfige Familie geplant wurde. Während die Gestaltung der Fassade nicht flexibel ist, kann das Innere aufgrund eines speziellen Raumaufteilungssystems und der Höhe der Räume eine Vielzahl von Raumgrößen beherbergen. Das Dach wurde aus Glasschindeln gefertigt, die auch für die Gestaltung einer Veranda, einer Galerie, die vom Hauptschlafzimmer wegführt, und einer Saunaterrasse verwendet wurden. Das Zentrum des Hauses ist ein doppelt hoher Bereich mit Wohnzimmer, Esszimmer und Küche.

Expuesta por vez primera en el año 2000 dentro de una feria sobre la vivienda en Finlandia, la Touch House es una vivienda prefabricada de 186 m² pensada para una familia de cuatro miembros. El diseño exterior no permite cambios, pero el interior admite variar el tamaño de los cuartos mediante un sistema de separación y la altura. La cubierta está compuesta de placas de cristal que crean un porche, una galería ante el dormitorio principal y una terraza con sauna. El centro de la casa lo forma un volumen de doble altura con el salón, el comedor y la cocina.

Exposée pour la première fois en 2000 dans une foire consacrée à l'habitat en Finlande, la Touch House est une maison préfabriquée de 186 m² conçue pour accueillir une famille de quatre personnes. Bien que le design extérieur ne soit pas flexible, l'intérieur peut abriter différentes tailles de pièces, selon un système de partition et la hauteur des pièces. Le toit est fait de plaques de verre qui créent une véranda, une galerie partant de la chambre principale et une terrasse sauna. Le centre de la maison est un volume de double hauteur qui comprend une salle à manger, un salon et une cuisine.

Esposta per la prima volta nel 2000 a una fiera di case in Finlandia, la Touch House è una casa prefabbricata di 186 m² quadri progettata per ospitare una famiglia composta da quattro persone. Mentre il progetto esterno non è flessibile, l'interno può ospitare una varietà di misure di camere, basandosi su un sistema di ripartizione e sull'altezza delle camere. Il tetto, che visto dall'alto ricorda la forma di una busta quadrata, è fatto di coperture in vetro che creano una veranda, una galleria come prolungamento della camera da letto ed una terrazza con sauna. Il centro della casa è un ambiente a doppia altezza che contiene un salone, una sala da pranzo ed una cucina.

DAVID HERTZ ARCHITECTS | SANTA MONICA (CA), USA

Website	www.studioea.com
Project	Panel House
Location	Venice (CA), USA
Building materials	Steel, concrete, prefabricated refrigeration panels
Photos	Juergen Nogai

This home's compact design requires that every available surface be used to achieve maximum sustainability and functionality. The angled walls create a view corridor to the ocean and allow prevailing breezes to flow through the house. The building exterior is made of prefabricated panels, typically used for walk-in refrigeration, that weigh less than one hundred pounds each and are 6 inches thick, 30 inches wide and 30 feet tall. The panels, which can be fastened by just two people, orient vertically with an interlocking joint and are screwed to the closure plate at the floors. Designed with a dull aluminium finish, the panels reflect the changing colors of the environment and create beautiful effects all year round.

Das kompakte Design dieses Hauses macht die Nutzung jeder verfügbaren Fläche erforderlich, um ein Maximum an Nachhaltigkeit und Funktionalität zu erreichen. Die winkeligen Wände bilden einen Panoramadurchgang zum Ozean, während sie gleichzeitig ein angenehmes Lüftchen hereinlassen, das durch das Haus weht. Die Gebäudefassade wurde aus Fertigelementen gefertigt, die üblicherweise für begehbare Kühlhäuser verwendet werden. Diese Elemente wiegen jeweils etwas weniger als 45 kg und sind 15 cm dick, 76 cm breit und 9 m hoch. Die Elemente, die von nur zwei Leuten befestigt werden können, werden mit einer Verfalzung vertikal ausgerichtet und mit dem auf dem Boden befindlichen Ausgleichsblech verschraubt. Durch ihr mattes Aluminiumfinish reflektieren die Elemente die wechselnden Farben der Umgebung und arrangieren wunderschöne Effekte während des ganzen Jahres.

Este compacto diseño requiere de toda la superficie disponible para conseguir el máximo de sostenibilidad y funcionalidad. Las paredes en ángulo crean un pasillo que mira directamente al océano y permite que la brisa recorra la casa. El exterior está hecho de paneles prefabricados -usados habitualmente para la refrigeración en abierto- con un peso inferior a los 45 kg cada uno y un grosor de 15 cm, 76 cm de ancho y 9 m de largo. Para fijarlos, bastan dos operarios. Los paneles se orientan verticalmente con una articulación y se atornillan a la plancha de cierre en el piso. El acabado en aluminio mate de los paneles refleja el color cambiante del entorno y crea espléndidos efectos durante todo el año.

Le design compact de cette maison requiert que toute la surface disponible soit utilisée pour obtenir une durabilité et une fonctionnalité maximales. Les murs inclinés créent un couloir avec vue sur l'océan et permettent aux brises dominantes de s'engouffrer dans la maison. L'extérieur du bâtiment est fait de panneaux préfabriqués, utilisés en général pour les chambres froides, qui pèsent moins de 45 kg chacun et mesurent 15 cm d'épaisseur, 76 cm de largeur et 9 m de longueur. Les panneaux, qui peuvent être fixés par seulement deux personnes, s'orientent verticalement avec un joint de verrouillage et sont vissés sur les plaques d'obturation des sols. Conçus avec une finition en aluminium mat, les panneaux reflètent les couleurs changeantes de l'environnement et créent de magnifiques effets toute l'année

Il progetto compatto di questa casa richiede che ogni superficie disponibile venga usata per raggiungere la massima sostenibilità e funzionalità. Le pareti ad angolo creano un corridoio con vista sull'oceano e consentono alla brezza di attraversare la casa. L'esterno dell'edificio è fatto di pannelli prefabbricati, di norma usati per la refrigerazione accessibile, che pesano meno di 45 kg ognuno ed hanno uno spessore di 15 cm, una larghezza di 76 cm ed un'altezza di 9 m. I pannelli, che possono essere fissati da due sole persone, sono orientati verticalmente con una giuntura di collegamento e sono avvitati alla piastra di chiusura sui pavimenti. Progettati con una rifinitura in alluminio leggero, i pannelli riflettono i colori mutevoli dell'ambiente e creano degli stupendi effetti per tutto l'anno.

DAN HISEL DESIGN | SOMERVILLE (MA), USA

Website   www.danhiseldesign.com
Project   Z-Box
Location   Lynn (MA), USA
Building materials   Perforated steel, translucent fiberglass
                     and douglas fir
Building manufacturer Continental Consolidated Industries
Photos   Peter Vanderwarker Photographs

This project is essentially a work of "Furnitecture": bed + shelves + closets + storage + lamp + dog's bed (!)= Z Box, a free-standing cube built inside a newly renovated, wide-open loft. The Z-Box solves two problems—Where to sleep? And where to store all the stuff?—through the act of merging, wherein the functions typically performed by several disconnected pieces of furniture are combined and distilled into a carefully carved block of perforated steel, polycarbonate, and douglas fir.

Dieses Projekt ist im wesentlichen ein Werk der „Furnitecture": Bett + Regale + Wandschränke + Abstellraum + Lampe + Hundekörbchen(!) = Z-Box. Die Z-Box ist ein freistehender Kubus, der innerhalb eines vor kurzem renovierten, weit offenen Lofts erbaut wurde. Die Z-Box löst zwei Probleme: Wo soll man schlafen? Und wo soll der ganze Kram hin? Die Lösung ist ein Verschmelzungsakt, wobei die typischen Funktionen mehrerer nicht zusammenhängender Möbel miteinander verbunden werden und in einem sorgfältig geschnitzten Block aus Lochblech, Polycarbonat und Douglasienholz „destilliert" werden.

Este proyecto consiste fundamentalmente en un trabajo de "Mobilitectura": cama + baldas + armarios + espacio de almacenaje + lámpara + cama del perro (!) = Z-Box, un cubo independiente construido en un loft diáfano recién reformado. Resuelve dos problemas: el de la zona de descanso y el del almacenaje. Este bloque cuidadosamente tallado de acero perforado, policarbonato y madera de abeto de Oregón combina funciones que normalmente cumplen elementos inconexos del mobiliario.

Ce projet est essentiellement un travail de "Meublitecture" : lit + étagères + placards + rangement + niche (!) = Z Box, un cube indépendant construit à l'intérieur d'un loft ouvert récemment rénové. La Z-Box résout deux problèmes – Où dormir ? Et où ranger toutes les affaires ? – grâce à l'art de la fusion : les fonctions habituellement remplies par plusieurs meubles sont combinées et distillées dans un bloc d'acier perforé, de polycarbonate et de douglas vert soigneusement sculpté.

Questo progetto è essenzialmente un lavoro di "Furnitecture" (architecttura di mobili): letto + ripiani + armadi + deposito + lampada + lettino per il cane (!)= Z Box: un cubo che si regge da solo costruito dentro ad un loft appena rinnovato e completamente aperto. La Z-Box risolve due problemi—Dove dormire? E dove riporre tutte le cose?—grazie ad un'azione di fusione, dove le funzioni normalmente svolte da diversi mobili disconnessi tra loro vengono combinate e condensate in un blocco scolpito con cura fatto di acciaio perforato, policarbonato e abete di douglas.

STEVEN HOLL ARCHITECTS | NEW YORK (NY), USA

Website	www.stevenholl.com
Project	Turbulence House
Location	Abiquiu (NM), USA
Building materials	Exterior: pre-constructed aluminum panels
	Cladding: natural finish Galvalum flat lock seam
Building manufacturer	Structural engineer: DeLapp Engineering
	Metal panel fabricator: A. Zahner Company
Photos	Andy Ryan

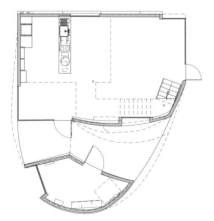

This small structure is situated atop a windy desert mesa. Its form, imagined to be like the tip of an iceberg that suggests a larger body below, allows the wind to blow through the center. The stressed skin and aluminum rib construction are digitally prefabricated then bolted together onsite. A total of 31 metal panels, each with an individual shape, form the unique "shell" of the house.

Diese kleine Konstruktion befindet sich auf einem Tafelberg in der Wüste. Die Form des Hauses soll an die Spitze eines Eisberges erinnern, der ein größeres Gebilde darunter vermuten lässt und dem Wind erlaubt, durch das Zentrum zu blasen. Sowohl die betonte Verkleidung als auch die Rippenkonstruktion aus Aluminium wurden digital vorgefertigt und schließlich vor Ort miteinander verschraubt. Insgesamt bilden 31 Metallelemente, jedes individuell geformt, die einzigartige „Schale" des Hauses.

Esta pequeña estructura se ubica en lo alto de una ventosa colina en el desierto. Su figura, semejante a la punta de un iceberg que hace pensar en la existencia por debajo de una masa mayor, posibilita el paso del viento por su interior. La construcción, de cubierta tensada de aluminio con nervaduras, se prefabricó de manera digital y se atornilló en destino. Un total de 31 paneles, todos diferentes, conforman el excepcional "caparazón" de esta casa.

Cette petite structure est située au-dessus d'une mesa déserte et venteuse. Sa forme, imaginée pour ressembler à la partie émergée d'un iceberg, permet au vent de passer en son centre. Les panneaux de revêtement à ailettes en aluminium sont préfabriqués numériquement puis assemblés sur place. Un total de 31 panneaux de métal, chacun d'une forme différente, forment la « coque » unique de la maison.

Questa piccola struttura è situata su un altopiano deserto e ventoso. La sua forma, immaginata come la punta di un iceberg che suggerisce una parte inferiore più ampia, permette al vento di soffiare attraverso il centro. Il rivestimento teso e la costruzione della gabbia in alluminio vengono prefabbricati digitalmente ed in seguito bullonati l'uno all'altro in sito. Un totale di 31 pannelli di metallo, ognuno con una forma individuale, formano l'eccezionale "guscio" della casa.

MASAHIRO IKEDA | TOKYO, JAPAN
ATELIER TEKUTO/YASUHIRO YAMASHITA | TOKYO, JAPAN

Website	www.miascoltd.net
	www.tekuto.com
Project	Lucky Drops
Location	Tokyo, Japan
Building materials	Structure: steel
	Exterior: fiber-reinforced plastic and electron beam film
	Interior: ceiling-curing sheet, floor and walls steel with
	anticorrosive, heat-insulation and waterproof treatments
Building manufacturer	Hideo Kikushima, Kikushima Co.,Ltd.
	Shigeki Matsuoka, Homebuilder Co.,Ltd.
Photos	Makoto Yoshida

Sleek and refined, this small home's design is defined by its long, narrow, trapezoidal shape. Utilizing the maximum length of the lot, the home slopes inside to make the best use of the underground space, turning the entire building into both a skin and a living area. The transparent walls allow sunlight to permeate throughout the interior while the expanded metal flooring allows light to fall deeper underground to the living quarters below. In short, every effort was made to create a place of living comfort.

Glatt und raffiniert, das Design dieses kleinen Hauses wird von seiner langen, engen, trapezartigen Form bestimmt. Weil die maximale Länge ausgenutzt wird, neigt sich das Haus innen, um die Untergrundfläche optimal auszunutzen, wodurch das gesamte Gebäude sowohl in eine Schale als auch in eine Wohnfläche verwandelt wird. Die transparenten Wände lassen das Sonnenlicht durch sämtliche Räume fluten, während der ausgedehnte Metallfußboden das Licht tiefer fallen lässt – bis in die Wohnbereiche darunter. Kurzum, es wurde alles Mögliche unternommen, um einen Ort mit Lebensqualität zu schaffen.

Esbelto y refinado, el diseño de esta vivienda está marcado por su alargada silueta, estrecha y trapezoidal. Aprovechando al máximo la longitud del solar, la casa se curva por dentro para un uso óptimo del espacio subterráneo, convirtiendo a todo el edificio tanto en cubierta como en zona destinada a vivienda. Las paredes transparentes dejan pasar al interior la luz y el piso de metal expandido permite que esta llegue a la zona de vivienda en el nivel inferior. En pocas palabras: todos los esfuerzos estuvieron encaminados a crear un lugar para vivir con todo el confort.

Elégante et raffinée, cette petite maison a un design défini par sa forme longue, étroite et trapézoïdale. En utilisant la longueur maximale de la parcelle, la maison s'incline pour utiliser au mieux l'espace souterrain, qui transforme tout le bâtiment en un espace à la fois de revêtement et de vie. Les murs transparents permettent à la lumière de passer à l'intérieur alors que les sols en métal déployé permettent à la lumière de s'enfoncer sous terre vers les espaces de vie au-dessous, tous les efforts ont été faits pour créer un espace de vie confortable.

Lucido e rifinito, il design di questa piccola casa è definito dalla sua forma lunga, stretta e trapezoidale. Utilizzando la massima lunghezza dell'appezzamento, la casa si inclina verso l'interno per utilizzare al meglio lo spazio sottostante, che trasforma l'intero edificio sia in una copertura sia in un'area abitabile. Le pareti trasparenti permettono alla luce del sole di penetrare all'interno, mentre la pavimentazione di metallo espanso consente alla luce di penetrare più in profondità negli alloggi sottostanti. In breve, ogni sforzo è stato intrapreso per creare un posto confortevole in cui vivere.

RAY KAPPE | SANTA MONICA (CA), USA

Website	www.livinghomes.net
Project	LivingHomes model 1.0
Location	Santa Monica (CA), USA
Building materials	Structure: recycled steel
	Forest Stewardship Council wood
Building manufacturer	Profile Structures Inc.
Photos	CJ Berg Photographics/Sunshine Divis

LivingHomes is a developer of modern, prefab homes. The company's homes are renowned for combining world-class architecture with an unparalleled commitment to health and sustainable construction. Designed by renowned architect, Ray Kappe, and constructed using natural and non-toxic materials and systems, the LivingHomes' model 1.0 home successfully marries style and substance. Located in Santa Monica, California, it is one of the first homes in the nation to achieve the LEED "platinum" certification, making it a leader in energy and environmental design.

LivingHomes ist ein Unternehmen, das moderne Fertighäuser entwickelt. Die Häuser der Firma sind bekannt für die Kombination von Weltklasse-Architektur mit einem beispiellosen Engagement in Bezug auf eine gesunde und umweltverträgliche Bauweise. Entworfen von dem bekannten Architekten Ray Kappe wurde das Haus unter der Verwendung von natürlichen und ungiftigen Materialien und Systemen konstruiert. Das LivingHomes model 1.0 vereint Stil erfolgreich mit Substanz. Es befindet sich in Santa Monica, Kalifornien, und ist eines der ersten Häuser der USA, das mit dem LEED Platin Zertifikat ausgezeichnet wurde, wodurch es an vorderster Front steht, wenn es um Energie- und Umweltdesign geht.

Livinghomes es un fabricante de modernas casas prefabricadas. Sus construcciones son famosas por combinar arquitectura de primer nivel mundial con un compromiso incomparable por construir de forma saludable y sostenible. Los diseños son del célebre arquitecto Ray Kappe. Emplean materiales naturales y no contaminantes. LivingHomes' model 1.0 aúna de forma lograda estilo y sustancia. Ubicada en Santa Mónica (California), es una de las primeras casas de EE. UU. que ha conseguido la certificación LEED de platino, convirtiéndolos en líderes en diseño energético y medioambiental.

LivingHomes est un fabricant de maisons préfabriquées modernes. Les maisons de cette compagnie sont renommées pour combiner une architecture de classe mondiale avec un engagement inégalé dans la construction saine et durable. Conçue par l'architecte renommé Ray Kappe et construite à base de matériaux et de systèmes naturels et non-toxiques, la maison LivingHomes' model 1.0 réussit le mariage entre forme et fond. Situé à Santa Monica, en Californie, c'est une des premières maisons du pays à obtenir la certification LEED « platine », ce qui en fait une pionnière en matière de design de l'énergie et de l'environnement.

LivingHomes elabora progetti di case moderne e prefabbricate. Le case di questa azienda sono rinomate per la loro capacità di combinare l'architettura di prima classe con un impareggiabile impegno per la realizzazione di costruzioni salutari e sostenibili. Progettata dal rinomato architetto Ray Kappe, e costruita usando materiali e sistemi naturali e non tossici, il modello 1,0 della LivingHomes sposa con successo stile e sostanza. Situata a Santa Monica, in California, è una delle prime case nel paese ad aggiudicarsi la certificazione LEED "platinum", diventando così leader nei progetti a risparmio energetico e rispetto dell'ambiente.

OSKAR LEO KAUFMANN, JOHANNES KAUFMANN | DORNBIRN, AUSTRIA

Website	www.olkruf.com
Project	FRED
Location	Reuthe, Austria
Building manufacturer	kaufmann zimmerei und tischlerei
Photos	Ignacio Martinez

FRED is a modular home-building system designed by architects Oskar Leo Kaufmann and Johannes Kaufmann that is as easy to combine and build as children's building blocks. Because the components of the mobile container system come in different sizes, they result in houses that differ in square footage, form, floor plan and detail. FRED can be expanded or contracted on-site. The exterior takes shape as the 16.5 x 16.5 foot modules are lined up or stacked on top of one another. Ten types of wall façades are available. Highly efficient organization enables the architects to offer short construction times and once on-site FRED can be fully assembled within just two hours.

FRED basiert auf einem Baukastensystem, das von den Architekten Oskar Leo Kaufmann und Johannes Kaufmann entworfen wurde. Es ist leicht zu kombinieren und zu bauen, praktisch in der gleichen Art, wie Kinder ein Haus aus Bauklötzen bauen. Weil die Bauteile des mobilen Containersystems in verschiedenen Größen angeliefert werden, entstehen daraus Häuser, die unterschiedlich sind in Bezug auf Fläche, Form, Grundriss und Detail. FRED kann vor Ort erweitert oder verkleinert werden. Sein Äußeres nimmt Form an, wenn die 5 x 5 m Module aufgereiht oder übereinander gestapelt werden. Zehn Arten von Fassaden sind lieferbar. Eine hoch effiziente Organisation ermöglicht kurze Konstruktionszeiten und wenn FRED erst einmal auf der Baustelle eingetroffen ist, kann es innerhalb von nur zwei Stunden komplett montiert werden.

FRED es un sistema modular habitacional diseñado por los arquitectos Oskar Leo Kaufmann y Johannes Kaufmann que es fácil de combinar y de ampliar, como las piezas de un juego de niños. Los componentes del sistema móvil de contenedores vienen en varios tamaños; de ahí resultan viviendas con superficies, formas, plantas y acabados distintos. FRED puede agrandarse o contraerse en su ubicación. El exterior toma la forma de los módulos de 5 x 5 m, según se dispongan en fila o se apilen. Se puede elegir entre diez fachadas diferentes. Una organización de lo más eficiente permite a los arquitectos construir en muy poco tiempo, y en tan solo dos horas, FRED se monta en su lugar de destino.

FRED est un système de construction immobilière modulaire conçu par les architectes Oskar Leo Kaufmann et Johannes Kaufmann, aussi facile à assembler et à construire qu'un jeu d'enfant. Parce que les éléments du système de container mobile sont de tailles différentes, ils permettent de créer des maisons qui varient en surface, forme, plan d'étage et détails. FRED peut être agrandi ou réduit sur site. L'extérieur prend forme quand on aligne ou qu'on empile les modules de 5 x 5 m. Dix types de façades sont disponibles. Une organisation extrêmement efficace permet à les architectes de proposer des temps de fabrication très courts et une fois sur site, FRED peut être assemblé en seulement deux heures.

FRED, progettato dagli architetti Oskar Leo Kaufmann e Johannes Kaufmann, è un sistema modulare di costruzione facile da combinare e costruire come le case di mattoni per bambini. Essendo i componenti del sistema di container mobile disponibili in varie misure, ne risultano case che si differenziano in superficie, forma, distribuzione e dettagli. FRED può essere espanso e contratto in loco. L'esterno prende forma quando i moduli di 5 x 5 m vengono allineati o impilati uno sull'altro. Sono disponibili dieci tipi di facciate. Un'organizzazione molto efficiente permette agli architetti di offrire tempi di costruzione ridotti: una volta in loco FRED può essere assemblata in sole due ore.

OSKAR LEO KAUFMANN, JOHANNES KAUFMANN | DORNBIRN, AUSTRIA

Website	www.olkruf.com
Project	SU-SI
Location	Reuthe, Austria
Building manufacturer	kaufmann zimmerei und tischlerei
Photos	Ignacio Martinez

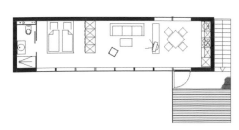

SU-SI mobile-home system was created in response to the firm's belief that conventional site-bound structures no longer fulfill contemporary needs and desires. SU-SI is a flexible structure that can be transported by truck, erected on-site, and installed within a period of five hours. It can even be placed on space-saving stilts to make room for a car underneath. It comes in different sizes, ranging in width from 10 to 11 ½ feet, and in length from 33 to 46 feet at a cost of around €36,000. Production can be completed within five weeks.

SU-SI ist ein mobiles Haussystem, das aus der Firmenvorstellung heraus geboren wurde, nach der konventionelle, baustellenabhängige Konstruktionen heutzutage nicht mehr den Bedürfnissen und Wünschen von Bauherren entsprechen. SU-SI ist eine flexible Konstruktion, die per LKW transportiert werden kann. Anschließend wird die Konstruktion vor Ort aufgestellt und innerhalb von fünf Stunden installiert. Sie kann sogar auf platzsparenden Pfählen errichtet werden, um Raum für ein Auto zu schaffen, das darunter abgestellt werden kann. Verschiedene Größen sind lieferbar: Die Breite liegt in einem Bereich zwischen 3 und 3,50 m, die Länge variiert zwischen 10 und 14 m, während sich die Kosten auf cirka 36.500 € belaufen. Die Produktion kann innerhalb von fünf Wochen fertig gestellt werden.

SU-SI es un sistema habitacional móvil que surgió como respuesta al convencimiento de que las estructuras fijas al uso habían dejado de satisfacer las necesidades y los deseos de hoy. SU-SI es una estructura flexible que se puede transportar en un camión y se levanta y se instala en el emplazamiento elegido en cinco horas. Se puede depositar incluso sobre unos soportes para ahorrar espacio y dejar sitio para el coche. Se presenta en diferentes tamaños, de 3 a 3,50 m de ancho y de 10 a 14 m de longitud, con un coste de unos 36.500 €. Para su producción se tardan cinco semanas.

SU-SI, un système de maison mobile, a été créé en réponse à la forte croyance que les structures traditionnelles liées à un site ne satisfont plus les besoins et les désirs actuels. SU-SI est une structure flexible qui peut être transportée par camion, montée sur site et installée en cinq heures. Elle peut même être installée sur des pilotis compacts pour former un garage sous la maison. Elle existe en différentes tailles, de 3 à 3,50 m de large, et de 10 à 14 m de long pour un prix d'environ 36 500 €. La fabrication peut être faite en cinq semaines.

SU-SI è un sistema di casa mobile, ed è stato creato in risposta alla convinzione dell'azienda che le strutture convenzionali legate al luogo di messa in posa non soddisfano più le esigenze ed i desideri moderni. La SU-SI è una struttura flessibile che può essere trasportata con un camion, eretta in loco ed installata in cinque ore. Può inoltre essere collocata su pilastri salvaspazio per creare un posto macchina nello spazio sottostante. È disponibile in varie misure, che variano in larghezza dai 3 ai 3,50 m e in lunghezza dai 10 ai 14 m ad un costo di circa 36.500 €. La produzione può essere completata nell'arco di cinque settimane.

KONYK | NEW YORK (NY), USA

Website	www.konyk.net
	www.up-house.com
Project	UP!house
Location	prototype, variable
Building materials	Structure: steel
	Façade: steel sandwich panels/fiberglass
Building manufacturer	konyk
Renderings	konyk

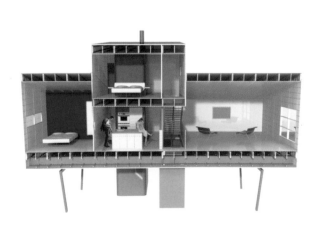

Originally commissioned by Dwell magazine, the UP!house is fashioned after design approaches that architect Craig Konyk discovered within the automotive industry. The result is a home that allows clients to choose from a range of options, including power windows and home theater entertainment packages. With its factory produced, lightweight steel tube construction, the home's frame is similar to an automobile "chassis," or frame. Utterly flexible, the home's parts can be re-assembled, allowing clients to add or remove elements as their needs change—or it can even be disassembled completely and moved to a whole new location.

Ursprünglich von Dwell magazine zusammengestellt, wurde das UP!house nach Designansätzen gestaltet, die Architekt Craig Konyk in der Automobilindustrie entdeckt hat. Das Ergebnis ist ein Heim, das dem Kunden ermöglicht, aus einer Reihe Optionen eine Auswahl zu treffen, inklusive Fensterheber und Pakete für die Heimkinounterhaltung. Wegen seiner fabrikgefertigten, leichten Stahlrohrkonstruktion hat der Rahmen des Hauses Ähnlichkeit mit dem Chassis oder Rahmen eines Fahrzeuges. Die Hausteile können völlig flexibel neu montiert werden, und die Kunden können je nach Wunsch und Bedarf Elemente hinzufügen beziehungsweise entfernen. Das Haus kann sogar komplett demontiert und an einen anderen Ort transportiert werden.

Up!House, en origen un encargo de la revista "Dwell", debe su diseño a las propuestas que el arquitecto Craig Konyk halló en la industria del automóvil. El resultado es una casa que ofrece a los clientes un amplio abanico de opciones que incluyen ventanas motorizadas o paquetes de cine en casa. El armazón de la casa, de tubo de acero ligero producido en una fábrica, se asemeja al chasis de un coche. Los elementos de esta construcción son extremadamente flexibles y se pueden volver a acoplar, por lo que el cliente puede retirarlos o añadir nuevos a discreción, y hasta puede desmontar la casa y llevársela a otra parte.

Commandée à l'origine par Dwell Magazine, l'UP!house est confectionnée selon les approches de design que l'architecte Craig Konyk a découvertes dans l'industrie automobile. Le résultat : une maison qui offre aux clients toute une gamme d'options, notamment des fenêtres automatiques et un pack home-cinéma. Avec sa construction en tubes d'acier léger fabriqués en usine, le cadre de la maison est similaire à un châssis automobile. Extrêmement flexibles, les parties de la maison peuvent être réassemblées, permettant aux clients d'ajouter ou d'enlever des éléments selon leurs besoins – la maison peut aussi être complètement désassemblée et déménagée vers un autre lieu.

Originariamente commissionata da Dwell magazine, la UP!house è stata modellata in base agli approcci progettistici appresi dall'architetto Craig Konyk nell'industria automobilistica. Il risultato è una casa che permette ai clienti di scegliere all'interno di una gamma di opzioni, tra cui finestre elettriche e home theater. Con la sua costruzione di tubi in acciaio, leggeri e prodotti in fabbrica, l'ossatura della casa è simile ad un "telaio" o ad un'ossatura di un'automobile. Completamente flessibili, i componenti della costruzione possono essere riassemblati, permettendo ai clienti di aggiungere o togliere elementi ogni qualvolta cambino le loro esigenze—o addirittura di smontare la casa completamente e spostarla in tutt'altro luogo.

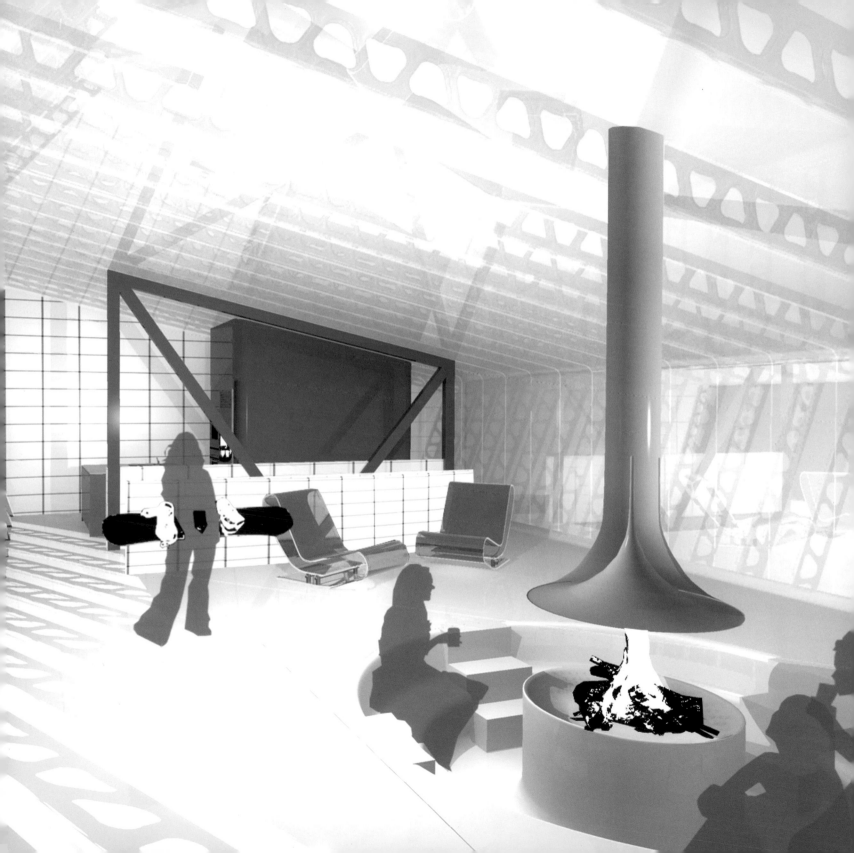

KORTEKNIE STUHLMACHER ARCHITECTEN | ROTTERDAM, THE NETHERLANDS

Website	www.kortekniestuhlmacher.nl
Project	'Las Palmas Parasite'
Location	Rotterdam, the Netherlands
Building materials	Walls, floors and roof: solid laminated timber panels made from European softwood
Building manufacturer	Finnforest Merk, Aichach/Christian Dörschug/ Jasper Kerkhofs
Photos	Anne Bousema, Errol Sawyer (p. 216 left), Rien Korteknie (p. 216 right)

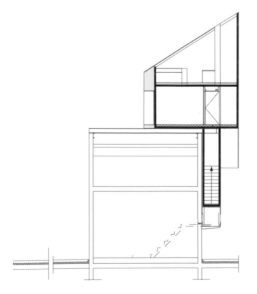

Developed for an international exhibition in 2001 that showcased parasitic uses of unused urban sites in Rotterdam, the Las Palmas Parasite was the only design built to full scale. A prototypical house combining the advantages of prefab technology and custom design, the house was designed for placement above the elevator shaft of a former warehouse building, so it required a compact site plan. The walls, floors and roof were made from solid laminated timber panels made from European softwood. The structure was precut to size and delivered on-site as a complete building package that took several days to install. Window frames were avoided by using a combination of fixed double glazing and openable timber shutters that celebrate the spectacular and highly varied views of new urban developments and harbour activities in the area.

Entwickelt für eine internationale Ausstellung im Jahr 2001, die parasitäre Nutzungen ungenutzter städtischer Grundstücke in Rotterdam demonstrierte, war Las Palmas Parasite der einzige Entwurf, der maßstabsgerecht gebaut wurde. Es handelt sich hier um den Prototyp eines Hauses, der die Vorteile der Fertighausbautechnologie und die Bedürfnisse des Kunden miteinander vereint. Das Haus sollte über dem Aufzugsschacht eines Lagerhauses platziert werden, daher benötigte man einen genauen Lageplan. Wände, Böden und Dach wurden aus soliden, laminierten Holzplatten gefertigt, die aus europäischem Weichholz bestehen. Die Konstruktion wurde größengetreu vorgeschnitten und als kompletter Bausatz auf die Baustelle geliefert. Für die Installation wurden einige Tage benötigt. Es wurde bewusst auf Fensterrahmen verzichtet, anstatt dessen verwendete man eine Kombination aus einer Doppelverglasung und zu öffnenden Holzfensterläden, die spektakuläre und häufig variierende Ausblicke auf neue städtische Entwicklungen und Hafenaktivitäten in der Gegend ermöglicht.

Diseñada para una exposición internacional en el año 2001, muestra un uso "parasitario" de emplazamientos urbanos abandonados en Rotterdam. El "Parásito de Las Palmas" fue el único diseño construido a escala 1:1. Un prototipo que combina las ventajas de la tecnología en prefabricados y el diseño por encargo, para ser emplazado sobre la caja del ascensor de un antiguo almacén, por lo que se necesitaba un buen plano de situación. Las paredes, los suelos y el tejado se hicieron de sólidos paneles laminados de maderas blandas europeas. La estructura se troqueló a medida y se envió a su destino en un solo paquete. Llevó varios días instalarlo. Combinando cristales dobles y postigos de madera, no se colocaron marcos en las ventanas, para así disfrutar de las espectaculares vistas del nuevo desarrollo urbano y de las actividades portuarias de la zona.

Créé pour une exposition internationale en 2001 qui montrait les utilisations parasites de sites urbains inutilisés à Rotterdam, le Las Palmas Parasite était le seul projet construit entièrement. Maison prototype combinant les avantages de la technologie préfabriquée et le design sur mesure, elle a été conçue pour être placée au-dessus de la gaine d'ascenseur d'un ancien bâtiment de stockage, et nécessitait donc un plan de situation compact. Les murs, les sols et le toit étaient faits de panneaux de conifère européen massif laminés. La structure a été prédécoupée à la bonne taille et livrée sur site dans un pack de construction complet qui a nécessité plusieurs jours d'installation. Les cadres de fenêtres étaient inutiles grâce à une combinaison de doubles-vitrages fixes et de volets en bois qui mettent en valeur la vue spectaculaire et très variée qu'offrent les nouveaux développements urbains et les activités portuaires de la zone.

Sviluppata per una mostra internazionale nel 2001 che presentava l'utilizzo parassitico di siti urbani inutilizzati a Rotterdam, Las Palmas Parasite è stato l'unico progetto costruito in misura reale. Una casa prototipo che ha combinato i vantaggi della tecnologia dei prefabbricati con un progetto personalizzato. La casa è stata progettata per essere posizionata sopra al vano ascensore di un edificio di un ex magazzino, ed era quindi necessario un piano compatto del sito. I muri, i pavimenti ed il tetto sono costituiti di solidi pannelli di legno dolce europeo laminato. La struttura è stata pretagliata a misura e consegnata in loco come un pacchetto di costruzione completo che ha richiesto diversi giorni per essere installato. Le cornici delle finestre sono stati evitate usando una combinazione di vetrate doppie fisse e persiane di legno apribili che celebrano le viste spettacolari e altamente varie dei nuovi sviluppi urbani e delle attività del porto nell'area circostante.

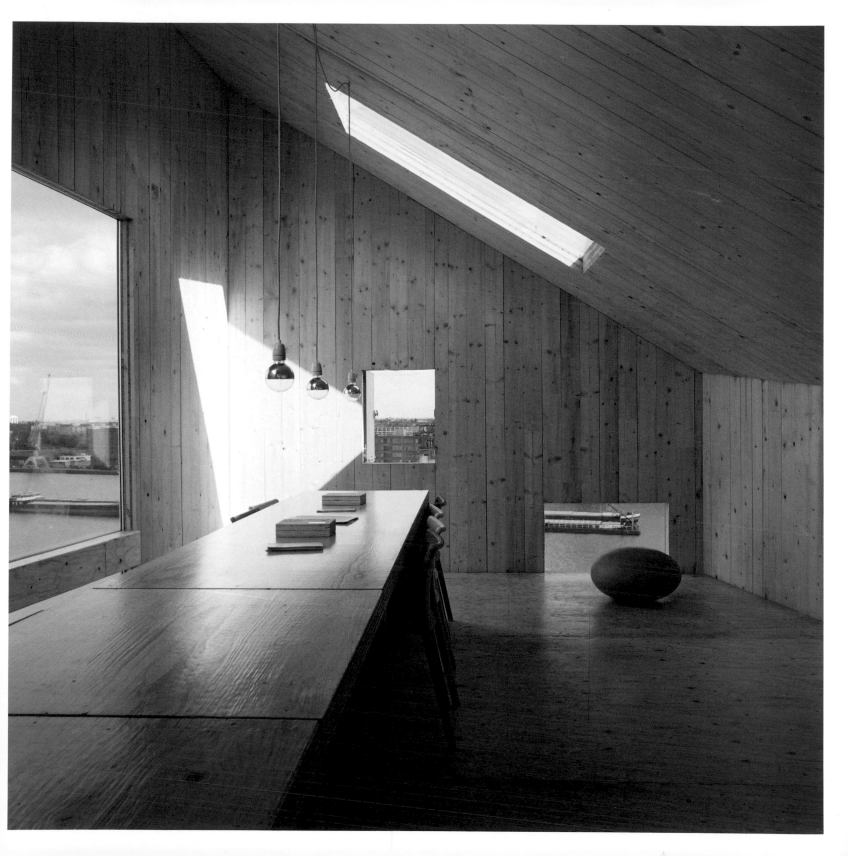

ROGER KURATH/DESIGN*21 | SANTA MONICA (CA), USA

Website	www.goDesign21.com
Project	Concrete Panel House
Location	Santa Monica (CA), USA
Building materials	Structure: steel frame
	Façade: concrete panels with integrated metal studs
Building manufacturer	Simple Building Solutions
Photos	Roger Kurath (p. 219), Robert Gregory

A **simple, contemporary home**, the Concrete Panel House's box-like design features an inner courtyard for privacy with small rooms fanning outward on all sides. The upper level houses a green roof-deck on which to enjoy surrounding views. The home's basic structure consists of a combination of steel frames, metal joists for the ceilings, and prefabricated concrete panels that act as the skin. Walls are prefabricated on-site and are the same size and take the same basic form. The home's sustainable features include a radiant heating system and dual glazed windows. Efficient and streamlined, the home is proof that prefabrication allows both architect and client the chance to create a custom home more efficiently and cost effectively than a conventionally built home.

Das simple, zeitgemäße Haus im kastenähnlichen Design setzt gekonnt einen Innenhof zum Ausruhen in Szene mit kleinen Räumen, die fächerförmig an allen Seiten nach draußen führen. Das obere Geschoss beherbergt eine begrünte Dachterrasse, von der aus man einen herrlichen Ausblick auf die Umgebung hat. Die Grundkonstruktion beseht aus einer Kombination von Stahlrahmen, Metallbalken zur Abstützung der Decken und vorfabrizierten Betonplatten, die als Verkleidung dienen. Die Wände werden vor Ort gefertigt und haben die gleiche Größe und Grundform. Zur Energieeinsparung tragen die Strahlungsheizung und doppelt verglaste Fenster bei. Das effizient aufzustellende Gebäude ist ein Beispiel für ein maßgefertigtes Heim, das kostengünstiger als ein konventionell gebautes Haus ist.

Una sencilla vivienda contemporánea, el diseño cúbico de la "Casa Panel de Hormigón" cuenta con un patio interior privado al que dan todas las pequeñas estancias. La planta superior dispone de azotea ajardinada desde la que disfrutar de las vistas. La estructura de la casa está compuesta por armazones de acero, viguetas de metal para los techos y paneles prefabricados de hormigón a modo de cubierta. La tabiquería es prefabricada in situ y tiene las mismas medidas y formas. En cuanto a la sostenibilidad, cuenta con calefacción radiante y ventanas de doble acristalamiento. Eficiente y de atractivas líneas, esta casa prefabricada demuestra que tanto arquitecto como cliente tienen la posibilidad de crear una casa a medida más eficiente y económica que una de construcción convencional.

Maison simple et contemporaine, la Concrete Panel House a un design en forme de boîte qui comprend une cour intérieure pour l'intimité, entourée de petites pièces. Le niveau supérieur abrite un toit-terrasse écologique sur lequel on peut profiter de la vue. La structure de base de la maison consiste en une combinaison de cadres d'acier, de poutrelles métalliques pour les plafonds et de panneaux de béton préfabriqués qui servent de revêtement. Les caractéristiques durables de la maison comprennent un système de chauffage à rayonnement et des fenêtres double-vitrage. Economique et dépouillée, la maison est la preuve que la préfabrication donne à la fois aux architectes et aux clients la chance de créer une maison personnalisée plus économique et écologique qu'une maison traditionnelle.

Una casa semplice e moderna, il progetto della Contrete Panel House, simile ad una scatola, comprende un cortile interno per la privacy con piccole stanze con ventilazione naturale su tutti i lati. Il livello superiore ospita una terrazza verde sul tetto dalla quale si può godere del panorama dei dintorni. La struttura di base della casa consiste in una combinazione di ossature d'acciaio, giunzioni metalliche per i soffitti e pannelli di cemento prefabbricati che fungono da rivestimento. Le pareti sono state prefabbricate in loco, sono di misura e di forma base uguali. Le caratteristiche sostenibili della casa includono un sistema di riscaldamento radiante e finestre con vetri doppi. Efficiente e semplificata, questa casa è una prova che la prefabbricazione offre sia all'architetto che al cliente la possibilità di creare una casa personalizzata più efficiente ed economica rispetto ad una casa costruita in modo convenzionale.

CHARLIE LAZOR, LAZOR OFFICE | MINNEAPOLIS (MN), USA

Website	www.lazoroffice.com
	www.flatpakhouse.com
Project	FlatPak house
Location	Minneapolis (MN), USA
Building materials	Danish cement board, powder coated aluminum, anodized aluminum, galvanized steel and recycled engineered cedar panel
Building manufacturer	Empyrean in Acton
Photos	Joel Koyama, Cameron Wittig (p. 230, 232)

The popular FlatPak house was designed, according to its creator designer Charlie Lazor, "to bring better space to more people." Essentially a menu of components, the system contains walls, cabinets, bathrooms, kitchen and built-ins. Since every site is different, FlatPak is endlessly configurable. Windows can be frosted or clear; an owner can opt for any number and configuration of spaces, from wide open and loft like to cozy, private get away rooms. Flatpak is one of the most critically acclaimed prefab houses available. It was chosen as one of the Top American Designs at the Smithsonian National Design Museum's "National Design Triennial." A 480 square-foot FlatPak house has toured North America with the Walker Art Center's prefab exhibit Some Assembly Required.

Das beliebte FlatPak house wurde laut seinem Schöpfer, dem Designer Charlie Lazor, entworfen, um „mehr Menschen bessere Räumlichkeiten zu ermöglichen". Tatsächlich beinhaltet es eine Auswahl an Bauteilen, Wänden, Schränken, Badezimmern, Küchen und Einbauten. Da jede Baustelle anders ist, ist das FlatPak endlos konfigurierbar. Die Fenster können aus satiniertem oder klarem Glas sein. Der Eigentümer kann jede Anzahl und Konfiguration in Bezug auf die Räume wählen; von weit offen und loftähnlich bis hin zu gemütlichen Räumen, in die man sich zurückziehen kann. Flatpak ist eines der hochgelobtesten Fertighäuser auf dem Markt. Es wurde anlässlich des „National Design Triennial" im Simthsonian National Design Museum zu einem der Topentwürfe Amerikas auserwählt. Ein 45 m² großes FlatPak House tourte mit der Walker Art Center Fertighausausstellung quer durch Nordamerika.

Según Charlie Lazor, diseñador de la popular FlatPak house, esta se concibió para "ofrecer un mejor espacio a más gente". En su lista de componentes, el sistema incluye básicamente tabiques, roperos, aseos, cocina y armarios empotrados. Puesto que cada emplazamiento es único, las posibilidades de configuración de FlatPak son infinitas. Las ventanas pueden ser de espejo o transparentes, el espacio interno puede configurarse diáfano como el de un loft o con habitaciones, acogedor e íntimo. FlatPak es una de las casas prefabricadas a la venta con mejores críticas. Fue elegido como uno de los mejores diseños americanos en el "Trienio de Diseño Nacional" del Museo Smithsonian de Diseño Nacional. Los 45 m² de esta casa han recorrido todos los EE. UU. con la exposición "Hay Que Montarla" del Centro de Arte Walter.

La très appréciée FlatPak house a été conçue selon son créateur, le designer Charlie Lazor, pour " apporter un meilleur espace à plus de gens". Basé sur un choix de composants, le système comprend des murs, des armoires, des salles de bains, des cuisines et des meubles encastrables. Comme chaque site est différent, FlatPak est configurable à l'infini. Les fenêtres peuvent être en verre dépoli ou transparent, le propriétaire peut choisir tout nombre d'espaces ou de configuration, de l'ouverture totale style loft aux pièces plus confortables et intimes. FlatPak est une des maisons préfabriquées les plus saluées par la critique. Elle a été choisie comme l'un des Top American Designs à la « Triennale Nationale du Design » du Smithsonian National Design Museum. Une maison FlatPak de 45 m² a fait une tournée en Amérique du Nord avec l'exposition de préfabriqués du Walker Art Center, Some Assembly Required.

Secondo il suo creatore, il designer Charlie Lazor, la famosa casa FlatPak è stata progettata, "per offrire spazi migliori a più persone". Si tratta essenzialmente di un menu di componenti: il sistema contiene pareti, armadi, bagni, cucine e mobili a muro. Dato che ogni luogo è diverso, FlatPak è configurabile all'infinito. Le finestre possono essere smerigliate o trasparenti; il proprietario può scegliere diverse quantità e configurazioni di spazi, dal completamente aperto stile loft, ad una composizione di stanze private ed accoglienti. La Flatpak è una delle case prefabbricate più applaudite dalla critica. E' stata scelta come una delle Top American Design alla "Triennale Nazionale del Design" presso il Smithsonian National Design Museum. Una casa FlatPak di 45 m² ha fatto il giro del Nord-America con la mostra del Walker Art Center intitolata "Some Assembly Required" ("E' Richiesto Un Po' di Assemblaggio").

LOT-EK | NEW YORK (NY), USA

Website	www.lot-ek.com
Project	lot-ek (CHK)
Location	prototype, variable
Building materials	ISO Shipping Container
Rendering	LOT-EK/Ada Tolla, Giuseppe Lignano, Keisuke Nibe

CHK (Container Home Kit) combines multiple shipping containers to build modern, intelligent and affordable homes. Forty-foot-long shipping containers are joined and stacked to create configurations that vary in size from approximately 1,000 to 3,000 square feet. Each container is transformed by using cutting sections of the corrugated metal walls. Joining the containers side by side, the layout allows for expanding the horizontal circulation, and thus the width of the container, to generate larger living spaces. The landscaping around the houses uses additional containers to configure a swimming pool, a pool house/tool shed and a carport.

CHK (Container Home Kit) kombiniert mehrere Versandcontainer miteinander, um moderne, intelligente und erschwingliche Häuser zu bauen. 12 m lange Versandcontainer werden miteinander verbunden und gestapelt, um Konfigurationen zu schaffen, deren Größen zwischen circa 93 bis 279 m² variieren. Jeder Container wird verwandelt, indem die Schnittstellen der Wellblechwände genutzt werden. Das Zusammenfügen der Container Seite an Seite erlaubt eine Erweiterung der waagerechten Auflage und damit auch der Breite des Containers. So entstehen größere Wohnräume. Für die Landschaftsgestaltung um das Haus herum werden zusätzliche Container genutzt, um daraus einen Swimmingpool, ein Poolhaus/Geräteschuppen und ein Carport zu zaubern.

CHK (Container Home Kit) utiliza diferentes contenedores navales para construir casas modernas, inteligentes y asequibles. Se ensamblan y apilan contenedores de 12 m de longitud dando lugar a configuraciones cuya superficie oscila entre los 93 y los 279 m². Cada contenedor se transforma por medio de piezas cortadas de las paredes de metal ondulado. Al unir los contenedores por las zonas ya recortadas, se expande la circulación horizontal, con lo que la amplitud del contenedor es mayor y, con ella, los espacios habitables. En el exterior también se emplean para configurar una piscina, una caseta para las herramientas o un garaje.

CHK (Container Home Kit) combine différents containers de livraison pour construire des maisons modernes, intelligentes et abordables. Les containers de 12 m de long sont assemblés et empilés pour créer des configurations qui varient en taille de 93 à 279 m². Chaque container est transformé grâce aux intersections des murs de métal ondulé. En unissant les containers côte à côte, la disposition découpée permet d'étendre la circulation horizontale, et donc la largeur du container, pour générer de plus grands espaces de vie. L'aménagement paysager autour des maisons utilise des containers supplémentaires pour créer une piscine, un abri de piscine/cabane à outil et un garage.

Il CHK (Container Home Kit) combina container da trasporto multipli per costruire case moderne, intelligenti ed economiche. Container da trasporto lunghi 12 m vengono giuntati ed impilati per creare composizioni distributive che variano tra i 93 a 279 m². Ogni container viene trasformato usando sezioni di taglio delle pareti di metallo ondulato. Saldando i container lato a lato, lo schema di ritaglio consente un'espansione orizzontale della circolazione e della larghezza del container, così da creare spazi abitabili più ampi. Container aggiuntivi sono utilizzati nel paesaggio circostante per configurare lo spazio della piscina, una tettoia ed un posto macchina.

MAE ARCHITECTS | LONDON, UK

Website	www.mae-llp.co.uk
Project	Lift-up house
Location	London, UK
Building materials	Flat pack cross-laminated structural timber panels, over-clad in a raincoat of Linnit profiled glass covering the structure with opaque glass shutters over the window
Photos	Killian O'Sullivan

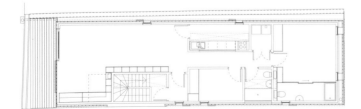

The **1070 square-foot glass box** sits on top of a converted factory building and provides living accommodation for the owners of the office below. Lift-up house intensifies a typical urban setting, leading to a high-density, mixed-use development; it provides a sustainable solution that can add life to a large number of similar small buildings in urban centers. The 2-bedroom house is constructed using a flat pack cross-laminated structural timber system and is clad in a raincoat of Linnit profiled glass. Opaque glass shutters over the windows allow the whole structure to be closed down for more privacy and security.

Der 100 m² große Glaskasten befindet sich auf einem ehemaligen Fabrikgebäude und schafft Wohnräume für die Eigentümer des darunter liegenden Büros. Das Lift-up house bereichert eine typisch städtische Kulisse, indem es zu einer dicht besiedelten, gemischt genutzten Entwicklung der Stadt beiträgt. Es bietet eine umweltfreundliche Lösung, die einer großen Anzahl ähnlich kleiner Gebäude in Ballungsgebieten zu mehr Wohnraum verhelfen kann. Für die Konstruktion des über zwei Schlafzimmer verfügenden Hauses wurde ein quer-laminiertes, strukturelles Holzsystem in Form eines Flachgehäuses verwendet. Das Haus wurde mit einem „Regenmantel" aus Linnit profiliertem Glas verkleidet. Durch blickdichte Fensterläden aus Glas über den Fenstern kann die gesamte Konstruktion geschlossen werden, so dass sowohl die Privatsphäre als auch die Sicherheit gewahrt werden.

Este poliedro de cristal de casi 100 m² se asienta sobre una antigua factoría reconvertida y sirve de hogar a los propietarios de las oficinas del piso inferior. La casa Lift-up es un ejemplo de un típico escenario urbano, densamente edificado, con desarrollo de usos mixtos, que representa una solución sostenible que puede dar vida a un buen número de edificios similares en los centros urbanos. Esta casa de dos dormitorios usa para su construcción un sistema estructural plano de madera de laminado cruzado impermeabilizado con cristal perfilado Linnit. Con los postigos de cristal opaco sobre las ventanas, la estructura puede cerrarse, ganando en privacidad y seguridad.

Cette boîte de verre de 100 m² est installée sur le toit d'un bâtiment industriel reconverti et fournit un hébergement pour les propriétaires du bureau au-dessous. La Lift-up house intensifie le cadre urbain, permettant un développement dense, à l'usage mixte : elle offre une solution durable qui peut donner un aspect plus vivant à un grand nombre de petits bâtiments similaires dans les centres urbains. La maison à deux chambres est construite grâce à un système de charpente en bois contreplaqué plat, et possède un revêtement imperméable en verre profilé Linnit. Des volets de verre opaques au-dessus des fenêtres permettent de fermer toute la structure pour plus d'intimité et de sécurité.

La cabina di 100 m² è posizionata sopra ad un edificio di una fabbrica trasformata e costituisce la residenza dei proprietari dell'ufficio sottostante. Lift-up house intensifica un'ambientazione urbana tipica, che porta ad uno sviluppo di alta densità e di utilizzo promiscuo. Fornisce una soluzione sostenibile che può aggiungere vita ad una vasta quantità di piccoli edifici simili nei centri urbani. La casa con due camere da letto è stata costruita usando un sistema di legno strutturato laminato incrociato ed è rivestita con un impermeabilizzante di vetro profilato Linnit. Delle persiane di vetro opaco sopra le finestre permettono all'intera struttura di poter essere chiusa per maggiori privacy e sicurezza.

MAE ARCHITECTS | LONDON, UK

Website	www.mae-llp.co.uk
	www.m-house.org
Project	m-house
Location	variable
Building materials	Insulated rigid steel frame and chassis with mill-finished corrugated aluminium exterior cladding and internal plywood lining
Photos	Morley von Sternberg

The appearance of the m-house—pronounced "mouse"—strongly reminds one of an oversized camper. Each of the two modules measures 10 feet in width (the maximum width permitted in traffic) and 56 feet in length. Only one day is required to build the prefabricated segments on the site. After installation, the m-house is ready for immediate occupancy. High-quality building materials, optimum insulation, and quality workmanship of the wooden, aluminum, and glass materials guarantee the longevity of the m-house.

Die Erscheinung des m-house, das wie „mouse" ausgesprochen wird, erinnert an ein überdimensioniertes Wohnmobil. Jedes der zwei Module misst 3 m in der Breite (entspricht der maximal zugelassenen Breite im Verkehr) und 17 m in der Länge. Es wird nur ein Tag benötigt, um die vorgefertigten Segmente auf der Baustelle zusammenzubauen. Nach der Installation kann das m-house sofort bezogen werden. Baumaterialien von höchster Qualität, eine optimale Isolierung und Qualitätsarbeit in Bezug auf die Materialien aus Holz, Aluminium und Glas garantieren die Langlebigkeit des m-house.

El aspecto externo de esta m-house – se lee como el inglés "mouse" (ratón) – recuerda enormemente a una caravana gigante. Cada uno de los dos módulos mide 3 m de ancho (lo máximo que permite el tráfico) y 17 m de largo. En un solo día se pueden ensamblar los elementos prefabricados. Después de la instalación, la m-house está lista para entrar a vivir. Materiales de construcción de primera, óptimo aislamiento y maderas, aluminio y cristal de gran calidad garantizan la longevidad de la m-house.

L'apparence de la m-house – prononcez "mouse" – évoque fortement celle d'une caravane démesurée. Chacun des deux modules mesure 3 m de large (le maximum autorisé sur la route) et 17 m de long. Il suffit d'un jour pour assembler sur site les segments préfabriqués. Après l'installation, la m-house peut être habitée immédiatement. Des matériaux de construction de grande qualité, une isolation optimale, et la facture de qualité des matériaux, bois, aluminium et verre, garantissent la longévité de la m-house.

L'aspetto della m-house—pronunciata "mouse"—ricorda fortemente quella di un camper smisurato. Ognuno dei due moduli misura 3 m di larghezza (la massima larghezza permessa in strada) e 17 m di lunghezza. E' necessario solo un giorno per la costruzione dei segmenti prefabbricati in loco. Dopo l'installazione la m-house è pronta per essere abitata subito. I materiali di costruzione di alta qualità, un ottimo isolamento ed i materiali in legno, alluminio e vetro, che vengono da una manifattura di ottima qualità e garantiscono la longevità della m-house.

MARMOL RADZINER | LOS ANGELES (CA), USA

Website	www.marmolradzinerprefab.com
Project	Desert House
Location	Desert Hot Springs (CA), USA
Building materials	Recycled steel frame modules
Building manufacturer	Marmol Radziner Prefab
Photos	Benny Chan Fotoworks, David Golmb (p. 257, 262)

The Desert House employs four house-modules and six deck-modules, a quantity chosen to suit the wide-open desert landscape. The desert climate inspired the architects to create covered outdoor living areas, and to develop sunshade modules to provide solar protection. By forming an "L," the home also establishes a protected, exterior environment that includes a pool and fire pit. The Desert House derives most of its power from solar panels, while sunshades on the south and west façades minimize the impact of the harsh summer sun. In colder months, concrete floors provide passive solar heat gain, making the home sustainable.

Das Desert House setzt vier Hausmodule und sechs Terrassenmodule ein. Diese Anzahl wurde gewählt, damit sich das Haus der weit offenen Wüstenlandschaft anpasst. Das Wüstenklima inspirierte die Architekten, überdachte Outdoor-Lebensräume zu schaffen und Sonnenschutzmodule zu entwickeln. Durch die L-Form des Hauses entsteht ein geschützter Außenbereich inklusive Pool und Feuerstelle. Das Wüstenhaus erhält seine Hauptenergie durch Solarkollektoren, während an den Fassaden im Süden und Westen befindliche Sonnenblenden die Einwirkung der extremen Sommersonne mindern. In kälteren Monaten erzeugen Betonböden passive Solarwärme, wodurch das Heim sehr umweltfreundlich ist.

La Desert House (Casa del Desierto) emplea cuatro módulos habitacionales y seis para el piso, cantidades elegidas para encajar en el extenso paisaje desértico. El clima del desierto sirvió de inspiración a los arquitectos para crear zonas exteriores cubiertas y desarrollar módulos con toldos para protegerse del sol. Con su forma de "L", la casa conforma un espacio exterior protegido que incluye piscina y un pequeño foso para hacer fuego. La mayor parte de la energía la obtiene de las placas solares. Los toldos al sur y al oeste minimizan el impacto del tórrido sol estival. En los meses más fríos, el suelo de hormigón almacena el calor del sol: una casa de lo más ecológica.

La Desert House utilise quatre modules-maison et six modules-terrasse, une quantité choisie pour s'accorder aux grands espaces du désert. Le climat du désert a inspiré les architectes pour créer des espaces de vie extérieurs, et pour créer des modules protecteurs contre le soleil. En formant un « L », la maison offre aussi un environnement extérieur protégé comprenant une piscine et un foyer. La Desert House obtient la majeure partie de son énergie de panneaux solaires, alors que les auvents des façades sud et ouest minimisent les effets de l'âpre soleil estival. Les mois les plus froids, les murs de béton fournissent un chauffage solaire passif, pour une maison durable.

La Desert House utilizza quattro moduli per la casa e sei moduli per la copertura, una quantità scelta per adattarsi al paesaggio completamente aperto del deserto. Il clima del deserto ha ispirato gli architetti a creare delle aree abitative all'aperto ed a sviluppare dei moduli parasole per fornire una protezione dal sole. Formando una "L" la casa definisce anche un ambiente protetto ed esterno che include una piscina ed una zona per il focolare. L'energia utilizzata dalla Desert House è in gran parte prodotta da pannelli solari. Mentre i parasole sulle facciate sud ed ovest minimizzano l'impatto dell'arido sole estivo, nei mesi più freddi i pavimenti di cemento forniscono un guadagno di calore solare passivo, rendendo così la casa sostenibile.

OFFICE FOR MOBILE DESIGN (OMD)/JENNIFER SIEGAL | VENICE (CA), USA

Website	www.designmobile.com
Project	Seatrain Residence
Location	Los Angeles (CA), USA
Building materials	Four recycled, 40 foot-long shipping containers
Building manufacturer	Seatrain Containers and Grain Trailers
Photos	Daniel Hennisy

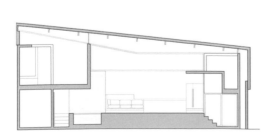

Four recycled, 40-foot-long shipping containers and two grain trailers make the modular components of this environmentally-conscious and affordable house. Not only do the industrial containers reflect the broader industrial landscape of the area, but additional materials, like wooden beams found on-site, were reused and integrated into the built project. The grain trailers were converted into a lap pool and indoor/outdoor koi pond. To designate living and work spaces, specific domestic functions were allocated to each storage unit. Large glass panels dramatically reconfigure the original vessels and allow natural light to puncture the interior, while also integrating the house within the context of the surrounding artists' community.

Vier recycelte, 12 m lange Versandcontainer und zwei Getreideanhänger bilden die Module dieses umweltbewussten und erschwinglichen Hauses. Nicht nur die Industriecontainer reflektieren die weitläufige, industriegeprägte Umgebung dieser Gegend, sondern auch zusätzliche Materialien wie Holzbalken, die auf der Baustelle gefunden und wieder verwertet wurden, indem sie in das Bauprojekt integriert wurden. Die Getreideanhänger wurden in einen Pool und einen Indoor/Outdoor Koiteich verwandelt. Um Lebensräume und Arbeitsräume festzulegen, wurden jeder Lagereinheit spezielle häusliche Funktionen zugeordnet. Großzügige Glaselemente gestalten die ursprünglichen Container grundlegend neu und erlauben dem natürlichen Licht den Innenraum zu durchbrechen, während so auch das Haus in den Kontext der Gemeinschaft der darum herum gruppierten Künstler integriert wird.

Cuatro contenedores navales reciclados de 12 m de longitud y dos tanques de grano componen los módulos de esta casa comprometida con el medio y asequible. No solo los contenedores reflejan el vasto paisaje industrial de la zona; otros materiales, como las vigas de madera que se encontraron en el propio emplazamiento, se reutilizaron e integraron en la construcción. Los tanques de grano se convirtieron en un estanque de olas y en otro interior y exterior para peces koi. Para dividir los espacios de vivienda y trabajo, se asignaron funciones domésticas específicas en cada unidad de almacenaje. Unos grandes paneles de cristal transformaron la configuración de los contenedores, permitiendo el paso de luz natural e integrando la casa en la vecina comunidad artística.

Quatre containers recyclés de 12 m de long et deux remorques à céréales sont les composants modulaires de cette maison écologique et économique. Non seulement les containers industriels reflètent le paysage industriel autour de la zone, mais des matériaux supplémentaires comme des poutres en bois trouvées sur place, ont été réutilisés et intégrés au projet de bâtiment. Les remorques à grain ont été transformées en une piscine pour la nage en longueur et un bassin à carpes intérieur/extérieur. Pour désigner les espaces de vie et de travail, les fonctions domestiques spécifiques ont été allouées à chaque unité de stockage. Des vastes panneaux de verre reconfigurent considérablement les cuves originelles et permettent à la lumière de percer à l'intérieur, ainsi que d'intégrer la maison dans le cadre de la communauté d'artistes.

I componenti modulari che costituiscono questa casa che rispetta l'ambiente ed è economica, sono quattro container riciclati e lunghi 12 m e due contenitori per il grano, Non sono solo i container industriali a riflettere il paesaggio industriale più ampio dell'area, ma anche i materiali aggiuntivi, come tronchi di legno trovati in loco, riutilizzati ed integrati nel progetto di costruzione. I contenitori per il grano sono stati trasformati in piscine sovrapposte ed in vasche koi per interno/esterno. Per definire gli spazi di soggiorno e di lavoro, sono state assegnate ad ogni unità di stoccaggio delle specifiche funzioni domestiche. Larghi pannelli di vetro riconfigurano drammaticamente i contenitori originali e permettono alla luce naturale di puntualizzare l'interno, integrando inoltre la casa nel contesto della vicina comunità di artisti.

OFFICE FOR MOBILE DESIGN (OMD)/JENNIFER SIEGAL | VENICE (CA), USA

Website	www.designmobile.com
Project	ShowHouse
Location	Venice (CA), USA
Building materials	Exterior: metal siding and translucent polycarbonate panels
	Interior walls: Kirei Board and Koskipanel
Building manufacturer	Brandall Modular
Photos	Benny Chan Fotoworks, Undine Pröhl (p. 279)

OMD's Prefab ShowHouse, a development of the Portable House, exhibits the ideas of prefabrication, flexibility, portability and compact spaciousness. Its central kitchen/bath core divides and separates the sleeping space from the eating/living space in a compact assemblage of form and function. The steel frame structure, measuring 12 x 60 feet, was trucked to its site and set on a temporary foundation. Its exterior is clad with metal siding and translucent polycarbonate panels, while its interior features a high sloping ceiling, iPort sound system, flowing ventilation, radiant heat panels, and a variety of sustainable floor and wall materials.

Das Fertighaus ShowHouse von OMD ist eine Weiterentwicklung des portablen Hauses und demonstriert die Idee der Fertigbauweise, Flexibilität, Portabilität und kompakter Geräumigkeit. Sein zentraler Küchen-/Badkern teilt den Schlafbereich vom Ess-/Wohnbereich in einer kompakten Kombination von Form und Funktion ab. Die Stahlrahmenkonstruktion, die 3,60 x 18 m misst, wurde per LKW zur Baustelle transportiert und auf einem temporären Fundament errichtet. Die Fassade ist mit einer Metallverkleidung und lichtdurchlässigen Platten aus Polycarbonat versehen, während die Innenausstattung durch eine hohe abgeschrägte Decke geprägt wird sowie einem iPort Sound System, Lüftungssystem, Strahlungswärmeelementen und einer Vielzahl an umweltfreundlichen Boden- und Wandmaterialen.

La casa prefabricada de OMD "ShowHouse", una evolución de la "Portable House" (casa portátil), expone las ideas de prefabricación, flexibilidad, portabilidad y amplitud compacta. La cocina/aseo central separa la zona de descanso de la del salón/comedor en una consistente articulación de forma y función. La estructura de acero, de 3,60 x 18 m, se llevó en camión hasta su emplazamiento y se depositó sobre cimientos provisionales. El exterior está revestido de metal aislante y paneles de policarbonato translúcido; el interior cuenta con techo inclinado, equipo de sonido iPort, ventilación de flujo, paneles de calefacción radiante y diversos materiales ecológicos en suelo y paredes.

ShowHouse, la maison préfabriquée d'OMD, est un développement de la Portable House, et présente les idées de préfabrication, de flexibilité, de transportabilité et d'espace compact. Son noyau cuisine/salle de bain central divise et sépare l'espace sommeil de l'espace vie/repas dans un assemblage compact de forme et de fonction. La structure cadre en acier, mesurant 3,60 x 18 m, a été transportée par camion sur site et posée sur des fondations temporaires. Son extérieur est revêtu de métal et de panneaux de polycarbonate translucide, alors que l'intérieur comprend un plafond pentu haut, une station d'accueil iPort, un système de ventilation, des panneaux de chauffage à rayonnement, et toute une gamme de matériaux durables pour les sols et les murs.

La ShowHouse prefabbricata della OMD, uno sviluppo della Portable House, mostra le idee di prefabbricazione, flessibilità, portabilità e ampiezza di spazio compatta. La cucina/bagno, sua anima centrale, divide e separa lo spazio notte dallo spazio giorno in una composizione compatta di forma e funzione. La struttura dell'ossatura in acciaio, che misura 3,60 x 18 m, è stata trasportata con un camion al luogo di messa in posa e posizionata su fondamenta provvisorie. Il suo esterno è rivestito con un rivestimento metallico e pannelli di policarbonato traslucido, mentre il suo interno comprende un soffitto alto ed inclinato, un impianto acustico iPort, un'abbondante ventilazione, pannelli di riscaldamento radianti ed una varietà di pavimentazioni e pareti sostenibili.

GEROLD PEHAM, DESIGN AND PLANNING | SEEKIRCHEN, AUSTRIA

Website	www.nomadhome.com
Project	Nomad Home
Location	variable
Building materials	Structure: steel with stone wool insulation (Klemmrock by Rockwool)
	Skin: aluminum, fiberglass, corrugated iron and larch wood
Building manufacturer	Fill Metallbau
Photos	Marc Haader

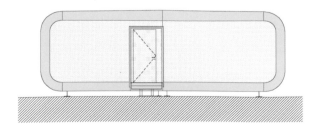

The Nomad Home is intelligently designed for maximum efficiency and flexibility. An ideal home for innovative and adventurous nomads, it can also serve as a coffee lounge, showroom or temporary office. The home's individual modules are easily extended, exchanged and modified. A specially developed iron skeleton ensures high tensile strength at low dimensions and allows for mounting and dismantling, as well as transporting the system several times without deformation. The exterior shell can be exchanged easily due to a simple connector system, and is available in various options. Based on a client's preference, it can arrive in a multitude of materials, including aluminum, fiberglass, corrugated iron and larch wood, among other choices.

Das Nomad Home wurde clever geplant, um maximale Effizienz und Flexibilität zu erzielen. Das ideale Heim für innovative und abenteuerlustige Nomaden kann auch als Kaffeelounge, Showroom oder temporäres Büro dienen. Die individuellen Module des Hauses sind leicht zu erweitern, auszutauschen und zu ändern. Ein speziell entwickeltes Eisengerüst garantiert hohe Zugfestigkeit bei niedrigen Abmessungen und ermöglicht das Montieren und Demontieren sowie den mehrmaligen Transport des Systems ohne Verformungen. Die Außenschale kann leicht ausgetauscht werden aufgrund eines simplen Verbindungssystems und ist in verschiedenen Ausführungen erhältlich. Je nach Wunsch des Kunden steht eine Vielzahl an Materialen zur Verfügung, wie zum Beispiel Aluminium, Fiberglas, Wellblech und Lärchenholz.

La Nomad Home (hogar nómada) tiene un diseño inteligente para alcanzar el máximo de eficiencia y flexibilidad. Es el hogar ideal para nómadas innovadores y aventureros; también puede funcionar como cafetería, sala de muestras u oficina provisional. Sus módulos individuales se pueden ampliar, permutar o modificar con facilidad. Un entramado de hierro garantiza una gran resistencia a las tensiones y permite montar la casa, desmontarla y transportarla sin deformarla. La cubierta exterior se cambia con facilidad gracias a su sencillo sistema de conexión. Si así lo desea el cliente, se puede fabricar en multitud de materiales, incluidos aluminio, fibra de vidrio, hierro ondulado y madera de alerce.

La Nomad Home a été intelligemment créée pour une efficacité et une flexibilité maximales. Maison idéale pour les nomades novateurs et audacieux, elle peut aussi servir de café, de magasin ou de bureau temporaire. Les modules individuels de la maison sont facilement agrandis, échangés ou modifiés. Un squelette de fer spécialement conçu assure une grande résistance à la traction avec des dimensions réduites et permet de monter et de démonter, ainsi que de transporter plusieurs fois le système sans le déformer. La coque extérieure peut facilement être échangée grâce à un simple système de connecteur, et est disponible en plusieurs options. Selon les préférences du client, elle peut être livrée dans une multitude de matériaux, notamment l'aluminium, la fibre de verre, le fer ondulé et le bois de mélèze.

La Nomad Home è progettata intelligentemente per dare massima efficienza e flessibilità. Una casa ideale per nomadi innovativi ed avventurosi, che può anche servire da bar, showroom o ufficio temporaneo. I moduli individuali della casa sono facili da estendere, scambiare e modificare. Uno scheletro in ferro elaborato appositamente per questo sistema, assicura una grande forza di trazione in ridotte dimensioni, e consente di montare, smontare e trasportare i moduli diverse volte senza deformarli. L'involucro esterno può essere cambiato facilmente grazie ad un semplice sistema di connettori ed è disponibile in varie opzioni e materiali secondo il gusto della clientela, tra cui l'alluminio, la fibra di vetro, il ferro ondulato ed il legno di larice.

RECETAS URBANAS, SANTIAGO CIRUGEDA | SEVILLA, SPAIN

Website	www.recetasurbanas.net
Project	Recetas Urbanas
Location	Barcelona, Spain
Building materials	Structure: steel
	Façade: a thin plate laminated with PVC, cellular polycarbonate, glass and a thin plate of aluminium-polythene
Photos	Recetas Urbanas

All components of this compact housing module are designed to stack and connect together to provide temporary living solutions on a plot of land. The building system is uniquely designed for easy and affordable transportation, assembly and expansion. The original housing solution is explored through the bold façade—a thin plate laminated with PVC, cellular polycarbonate, glass, and a thin plate of aluminium-polythene.

Sämtliche Komponenten dieses kompakten Hausmoduls wurden entworfen, um gestapelt und miteinander verbunden zu werden, so dass temporäre Wohnlösungen auf einem Grundstück geschaffen werden können. Das Konstruktionssystem wurde einzig und allein für den einfachen und erschwinglichen Transport, die Montage und Erweiterung entworfen. Die originelle Wohnlösung wird durch die kühne Fassade offensichtlich: Eine dünne, PVC-laminierte Platte, netzförmiges Polycarbonat, Glas und eine dünne Platte aus Aluminium-Polyethylen.

Todos los componentes de este módulo habitacional compacto están diseñados para poder apilarse y conectarse unos con otros para ofrecer cobijo temporal en un solar. El sistema tiene un diseño único que facilita y abarata su transporte, montaje y ampliación. Esta solución habitacional tan original viene marcada por su atrevida fachada: una delgada plancha laminada con PVC, policarbonato celular, vidrio y una fina plancha de aluminio-politeno.

Tous les composants de ce module de logement compact sont conçus pour être empilés et connectés pour fournir des solutions de d'hébergement temporaire sur une parcelle de terrain. Le système de construction est conçu de manière unique pour un transport, un assemblage et une extension faciles et abordables. Cette solution de logement originale s'exprime dans la façade audacieuse – une fine plaque de couches de PVC, de polycarbonate cellulaire et de verre, et une fine plaque d'aluminium-polyéthylène.

Tutti i componenti di questo modulo abitativo compatto sono progettati per essere impilati e connessi l'uno all'altro e per offrire soluzioni abitative temporanee su un appezzamento di terra. Questo unico sistema costruttivo è progettato con l'obiettivo di rendere il trasporto, l'assemblaggio e l'espansione facili ed economici. La soluzione abitativa originale viene esplorata tramite l'audace facciata—una sottile piastra laminata con PVC, policarbonato cellulare, vetro e una sottile piastra di alluminio-polietilene.

RESOLUTION 4: ARCHITECTURE | NEW YORK (NY), USA

Website	www.re4a.com
Project	Country Retreat
Location	The Plains (VA), USA
Building materials	Horizontal cedar siding, cement board panels and standing seam metal roof
Building manufacturer	Apex Homes
Photos	Resolution 4: Architecture (p. 293), Stephen Waudby

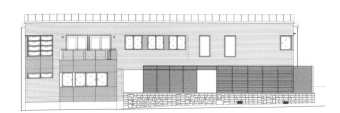

The Country Retreat takes advantage of its beautiful location within the countryside of Virginia. The design emphasizes the distant mountain views and natural light through plentiful windows and generously sized decks off the front and rear facades. To meet the client's need for a liveable floor plan and a well-orchestrated flow of space, the ground floor is an open plan module containing a living room, dining area and a kitchen, which can be entirely open to the paved outdoor pool area or enclosed by a curtain. More private spaces, such as bedrooms and guest suites, make up the second story volume of the home. For both security and privacy issues, the limestone paved pool area can be completely closed to the exterior with a series of stone walls and 2 x 2 cedar slated gate and fence system.

Le Country Retreat tire parti de son magnifique emplacement dans la campagne de Virginie. Le design souligne sur la vue sur les montagnes au loin et la lumière naturelle grâce à de nombreuses fenêtres et de spacieuses terrasses à l'avant et à l'arrière du bâtiment. Pour répondre au besoin du client d'avoir un plan d'étage vivable et un espace bien orchestré, le rez-de-chaussée est un module au plan ouvert comprenant un salon, une salle à manger et une cuisine. Les espaces plus privés, comme les chambres et suites d'invités, composent le volume du premier étage de la maison. Pour des questions de sécurité et d'intimité, la zone entourant la piscine, pavée en calcaire, peut être complètement fermée à l'extérieur avec des murs de pierre et un système de clôture et de barrières en latte de cèdre 2 x 2.

Das Country Retreat profitiert von seiner wunderschönen, ländlichen Lage in Virginia. Das Design des Hauses betont den Blick auf die entfernt liegenden Berge und den Tageslichteinfluss durch reichlich Fenster und großzügig gestaltete Terrassen vor und hinter dem Haus. Um dem Wunsch des Bauherrn nach einem lebenswerten Grundriss und reichlich Platz gerecht zu werden, stellt das Erdgeschoss ein offenes Modul dar, das ein Wohnzimmer, Essbereich und eine Küche beherbergt. Dieses Modul kann komplett zum gepflasterten Outdoor-Pool geöffnet oder durch einen Vorhang abgetrennt werden. Ein weiterer privater Bereich wie zum Beispiel Schlaf- und Gästezimmer bilden das zweite Geschoss des Hauses. Zur Sicherheit und zum Schutz der Privatsphäre kann der mit Kalkstein gepflasterte Poolbereich durch eine Reihe Steinmauern und ein 2 x 2 Tor- und Zaunsystem aus Zedernholz vollständig von der Außenwelt abgeschirmt werden.

Il Country Retreat gode di una bellissima posizione nella campagna della Virginia. Il progetto enfatizza la vista delle montagne distanti e la luce naturale attraverso abbondanti finestre e grandi terrazze sulle facciate del fronte e del retro. Per venire incontro alle esigenze del cliente di una pianta vivibile ed un flusso di spazio ben orchestrato, il piano terra è un modulo a pianta aperta che contiene il salone, l'area da pranzo e la cucina, che possono essere chiuse da una tenda o completamente aperte verso l'area esterna pavimentata della piscina. Gli spazi più privati, come le camere da letto e gli appartamenti per gli ospiti, compongono la seconda parte della casa. Per una questione di sicurezza e privacy, l'area della piscina pavimentata con calcare può essere completamente chiusa verso l'esterno con una serie di muri in pietra e un sistema di recinti e cancelli fissati con cedro 2 x 2.

Este "retiro campestre" saca partido de la belleza de su emplazamiento en el campo de Virginia. El diseño pone de relieve las vistas a las montañas distantes, la luz natural que atraviesa las ventanas y las generosas terrazas ante las fachadas anterior y posterior. Para satisfacer al cliente que busca un plano atractivo y una distribución del espacio bien orquestada, la planta baja es diáfana y cuenta con sala de estar, comedor y cocina, que se puede abrir a la zona pavimentada de la piscina o cerrar con una cortina. Espacios privados tales como los dormitorios y los cuartos de invitados conforman la segunda planta. Por cuestiones de seguridad y privacidad, la zona pavimentada con piedra caliza de la piscina se puede cerrar por completo al exterior con una serie de tabiques de piedra, una doble compuerta de madera de cedro de 2 x 2 y un vallado.

RESOLUTION 4: ARCHITECTURE | NEW YORK (NY), USA

Website	www.re4a.com
Project	Mountain Retreat
Location	Kerhonkson (NY), USA
Building materials	Horizontal cedar siding, cement board panels, standing seam metal roof and cedar decking
Building manufacturer	Apex Homes
Photos	floto+warner

Located on a five-acre rocky outcrop in the Catskills, the Mountain Retreat is a carefully crafted 1,800 square-foot home that accommodates ample indoor and outdoor living space. Comprised of three modules and a saddle, the home sits atop the ground floor module and projects outward onto concrete pilings. Its angular lines, soaring height, and unique blend of warm cedar siding with cool gray concrete panels and glass, anchors the modern dwelling within the rough mountaintop setting. An enclosed staircase runs along the north side of the house sheathed with grey Cembonit, and leads from the ground floor entrance to the main living spaces above, which sit peacefully among the treetops.

Auf einem 20.000 m² großen felsigen Aufschluss in den Catskills gelegen, ist das Mountain Retreat ein sorgfältig verarbeitetes 167 m² großes Haus, das einen großzügigen Indoor- und Outdoor-Lebensraum beherbergt. Bestehend aus drei Modulen und einem Sattel, befindet sich das Heim auf einem Erdgeschossmodul und ragt auf Betonpfeilern nach außen. Seine winkeligen Linien, die rapide zunehmende Höhe und eine einzigartige Mischung aus warmer Zedernholzverkleidung, kühlen grauen Betonplatten und Glas, verankern das moderne Wohnhaus mit der rauen Kulisse der Bergspitze. Ein abgeschlossenes Treppenhaus verläuft längs der Nordseite des Hauses, ummantelt von grauem Cembonit. Es führt vom Eingang im Erdgeschoss zu den oberen Hauptwohnräumen, die ruhig und friedlich zwischen den Baumkronen eingebettet sind.

Situada sobre un cerro rocoso de unos 20 000 m² en las montañas Catskills cercanas a Nueva York, Mountain Retreat (retiro en la montaña) es una casa de 167 m² construida con esmero y que dispone de mucho espacio interior y exterior. Se compone de tres módulos y una plataforma, la vivienda se asienta sobre el módulo a ras de suelo y se proyecta sobre pilares de hormigón. Sus aristas, sus grandes alturas y una extraordinaria combinación de cubierta de cedro con paneles de hormigón gris y cristal, integran este moderno hogar con el agreste marco montañoso. Una escalera cerrada atraviesa la zona norte recubierta con Cembonit gris y enlaza la entrada de la planta baja con las tranquilas áreas de vivienda de la planta superior, rodeadas por las copas de los árboles.

Située sur un affleurement rocheux de 20.000 m² dans les Catskills, la Mountain Retreat est une maison de 167 m² qui accueille un large espace de vie intérieur et extérieur. Composée de trois modules et d'un perron, la maison est au-dessus du module de rez-de-chaussée et se projette à l'extérieur sur des piliers en béton. Ses lignes anguleuses, sa grande hauteur et son mélange unique de revêtements en cèdre chaud et de panneaux de béton gris froid et de verre, ancre cette habitation moderne dans son rude cadre montagnard. Une cage d'escalier fermée court le long de la façade nord de la maison, recouverte de Cembonit gris, et mène de l'entrée du rez-de-chaussée aux espaces de vie principaux au-dessus, paisiblement installés au milieu des cimes des arbres.

Situata su una pendice rocciosa di 20.000 m² nelle Catskills, il Mountain Retreat è una casa che, realizzata con cura artigianale, misura 167 m² ed ospita un ampio spazio abitativo interno ed esterno. Composta di tre moduli ed una piattaforma, la casa è collocata sopra al modulo del piano terra e si proietta verso l'esterno su pilastri di cemento. Le sue linee angolari, la sua grande altezza e la sfumatura unica del suo rivestimento in cedro unita al freddo grigio dei pannelli di cemento e vetro, ancorano l'abitazione moderna all'ambientazione cruda della cima della montagna. Una scala chiusa rivestita con Cembonit grigio corre lungo il lato nord della casa, e porta dall'ingresso del piano terra agli spazi abitativi principali superiori che giacciono pacificamente in mezzo alle cime degli alberi.

RESOLUTION 4: ARCHITECTURE | NEW YORK (NY), USA

Website	www.re4a.com
Project	The Dwell Home
Location	Pittsboro (NC), USA
Building materials	Exterior: horizontal cedar siding, cement board panels, standing seam metal roof and recycled wood composite decking
Building manufacturer	Carolina Building Solutions
Photos	Resolution 4: Architecture (p. 308 left, right top, 309), Roger Davies

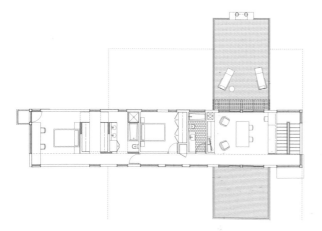

The winning entry of the Dwell Home Design Invitational, this popular prefab home is comprised of five prefabricated modules that equal 2,042 square feet. Regarded as the leader in superior, prefabricated building technology, the Dwell Home's compact and efficient quarters offer large open living spaces with a master bedroom at one end of the volume, and two bathrooms and an office that run along the same axis. Since approximately 80% of the house was built in a factory, the construction process leveraged the efficiency of wood framed modules, and the time required of crews on-site was significantly diminished. This, in turn, minimized the environmental impact on the local ecosystems, including the waste that is typically deposited on or near the site, and the transport of crews and materials.

Sieger der Dwell Home Design Invitational wurde dieses beliebte Fertighaus, das sich aus fünf vorgefertigten Modulen zusammen setzt, die 190 m² ausmachen. Das Dwell Home, das in Bezug auf anspruchsvolle Fertigbauweise als führend betrachtet wird, bietet mit kompakten und effizienten Vierteln große Wohnräume mit einem großen Schlafzimmer an einem Ende des Komplexes und zwei Bädern und einem Büro, die sich über die gesamte Achse erstrecken. Da circa 80% des Hauses in einer Fabrik gefertigt wurden, setzte der Bauprozess wirksam die Effizienz von Holzrahmenmodulen ein, so dass die Zeit, die die Bautrupps auf der Baustelle anwesend sein mussten, erheblich reduziert werden konnte. Dadurch wurde wiederum die umwelttechnische Auswirkung auf die örtlichen Ökosysteme auf ein Minimum reduziert. Auch der Abfall, der üblicherweise direkt auf der Baustelle oder in der Nähe der Baustelle entsorgt wird, und der Transport der Bautrupps und der Materialien konnten minimiert werden.

La vencedora del certamen de diseño de viviendas de Dwell fue esta popular casa compuesta por cinco módulos prefabricados que suman un total de 190 m². Se la considera la máxima expresión en tecnología de construcciones prefabricadas. Sus dependencias, amplias, compactas y eficientes, cuentan con un gran dormitorio en un extremo del volumen y con dos baños y un despacho que se extienden por le mismo eje. Puesto que un 80% de la casa se construyó en fábrica, la obra puso de manifiesto la eficacia de los módulos de armazón de madera. El tiempo que se empleó en montarla fue significativamente menor, lo que redujo el impacto ambiental sobre el ecosistema local, incluyendo los desechos –que suelen depositarse en el lugar de trabajo o cerca de él– y el transporte de operarios y material.

Lauréate du Dwell Home Design Invitational, cette maison préfabriquée appréciée comprend cinq modules préfabriqués d'une surface totale de 190 m². Considérée comme leader dans la technologie du bâtiment préfabriqué de qualité supérieure, la Dwell Home possède des parties compactes et économes qui offrent de larges espaces de vie avec une grande chambre à un bout du volume, et deux salles de bain et un bureau le long du même axe. Comme environ 80% de la maison est construit en usine, le processus de construction tire profit des modules encadrés de bois, et le temps requis sur site pour le personnel est considérablement diminué. Cela permet, par ailleurs, de minimiser les effets négatifs sur les écosystèmes locaux, notamment les déchets qui sont habituellement déposés sur le site ou à proximité, et le transport du personnel et des matériaux.

Articolo vincente della Dwell Home Design Invitational, questa famosa casa prefabbricata è composta da cinque moduli prefabbricati per un totale di 190 m². Considerati leader nella tecnologia superiore di costruzione prefabbricata, gli alloggi compatti ed efficienti della Dwell Home offrono degli ampi spazi abitativi aperti con una camera da letto principale ad una estremità del volume, e due camere da letto ed un ufficio lungo lo stesso asse. Considerato che circa l'80% della casa è stato costruito in una fabbrica, il processo di costruzione utilizza abilmente i moduli incorniciati di legno riducendo significativamente il tempo impegnato dagli addetti. Questo, di conseguenza, minimizza l'impatto ambientale sugli ecosistemi locali, inclusi i rifiuti che vengono di norma deposti su o vicino al sito e il trasporto di addetti e materiali.

ROCIO ROMERO | PERRYVILLE (MO), USA

Website	www.rocioromero.com
Project	LV Home
Location	Perryville (MO), USA
Building materials	Exterior shell kit package: post and beam, exterior wall panels, faux wall panels, roof framing, select connectors, and siding material
Building manufacturer	Rocio Romero LLC.
Photos	Richard Sprengler

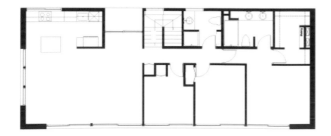

Designed and manufactured by Rocio Romero, the LV series has been created to enhance a modern lifestyle that is connected to nature. This second LV prototype is built on-site with factory-built kit components. All of the units have a standard width of 25 feet and one inch, but vary in size because of the differences in length. Three standard types of foundations are offered: crawlspace, basement, and/or slab on grade. Each unit can be customized to meet specific needs and tastes; there are several exterior siding options as well as various interior and exterior wall configurations.

Conçue et fabriquée par Rocio Romero, la série LV a été créée pour exalter un style de vie moderne en connexion avec la nature. Ce second prototype LV est construit sur site avec des éléments manufacturés en kit. Toutes les unités ont une largeur standard de 8 025 m, mais varient en longueur. Trois types de fondation standards sont proposés : vide sanitaire, sous-sol et/ou dalle sur le sol. Chaque unité peut être personnalisée pour répondre à des besoins ou des goûts spécifiques : de nombreuses options de revêtement extérieur ainsi que différentes configurations de murs intérieurs et extérieurs sont proposées.

Die LV Serie, entworfen und gefertigt von Rocio Romero, wurde kreiert, um einen modernen, naturverbundenen Lebensstil zu fördern. Dieser zweite LV Prototyp wird vor Ort aus fabrikgefertigten Baukastenelementen gefertigt. Alle Einheiten haben eine Standardbreite von 8.025 m, variieren jedoch in der Größe aufgrund der Längenunterschiede. Es werden drei Standardfundamenttypen angeboten: Kriechraum, Keller und/oder eine bodengleiche Fundamentplatte. Jede Einheit kann kundenspezifisch je nach Wunsch und Geschmack gefertigt werden. Es gibt mehrere Optionen in Bezug auf die Außenverkleidung sowie verschiedene Innen- und Außenwandstrukturen.

Progettata e prodotta da Rocio Romero, la serie LV è stata creata per accrescere uno stile di vita moderno che sia connesso alla natura. Questo secondo prototipo LV è costruito in loco con un pacchetto di componenti costruiti in fabbrica. Tutte le unità hanno una larghezza standard di 8.025 m, ma variano in grandezza a causa delle differenti lunghezze. Vengono offerti tre tipi di fondamenta: a passo d'uomo, basamento, e/o lastra su livello. Ogni unità può essere personalizzata per venire incontro alle esigenze e ai gusti specifici; esistono diverse opzioni per i rivestimenti esterni oltre a varie combinazioni per le pareti interne ed esterne.

Diseñada y fabricada por Rocío Romero, la serie LV se creó para acentuar un estilo de vida moderno vinculado con la naturaleza. Este segundo prototipo de LV se levantó en su emplazamiento definitivo con componentes manufacturados en fábrica. Todas las unidades tienen un grosor de 8.025 m, pero su tamaño varía en función de la longitud. Se ofertan tres tipos de cimentación: con acceso, con sótano o cubierto con plancha. Cada unidad puede personalizarse según las necesidades y gustos. Se puede elegir entre varios aislantes exteriores y diferentes configuraciones de la tabiquería interna y externa.

SOHO ARCHITEKTUR UND STADTPLANUNG | MEMMINGEN, GERMANY

Website	www.soho-architektur.de
Project	Haus Sunoko
Location	Memmingen, Germany
Building materials	Exterior clad in corrugated plexiglass panels
Photos	Rainer Retzlaff

An unusual property size of 755 feet long by 33 feet wide, and a very lean cost-calculation were the decisive factors in the design form of the "house on stilts." The gorgeous panoramas of the farms, fields and gardens were considered when drawing up the floor plan. There are large wooden openings in the façade of the two-story building, which is clad in corrugated, plexiglas panels. The floor, exterior walls, and ceiling elements are completely ready-made for the modular building, allowing the house to be completed in a single day.

Ein außergewöhnliches Anwesen mit einem Unfang von 230 m Länge und 10 m Breite sowie eine sehr knappe Kostenkalkulation waren die entscheidenden Faktoren in Bezug auf die Form des „Hauses auf Pfählen". Das atemberaubende Panorama der Bauernhöfe, Felder und Gärten wurde mit ins Kalkül gezogen, als der Grundriss gezeichnet wurde. In der mit geriffelten Plexiglasplatten verkleideten Fassade des zweigeschossigen Gebäudes befinden sich große Öffnungen. Der Boden, die Außenwände und die Deckenelemente wurden komplett für die Baukastensystembauweise vorgefertigt, so dass das Haus innerhalb nur eines einzigen Tages fertig gestellt werden kann.

Un inmueble de medidas poco convencionales (230 m de largo por 10 m de ancho) y un presupuesto muy ajustado fueron los factores decisivos a la hora de diseñar esta "casa sobre pilotes". La imponente vista sobre granjas, campos y huertos se tuvo en cuenta en el diseño del plano. La fachada de esta edificación de dos plantas cuenta con grandes vanos de madera y está recubierta con paneles de plexiglás ondulado. El piso, las paredes exteriores y los elementos del techado se prefabricaron para esta construcción modular, lo que permitió montarla en un solo día.

Une propriété d'une taille inhabituelle de 230 m de long sur 10 m de large, et un calcul des coûts très serré, ont été les facteurs décisifs pour le choix de la forme de la « maison sur pilotis ». La magnifique vue sur les fermes, les champs et les jardins a été prise en compte pour le dessin du plan d'étage. La façade de ce bâtiment sur deux niveaux, couverte de panneaux de plexiglas ondulés, offre de larges ouvertures en bois. Le sol, les murs extérieurs et les éléments de plafond sont déjà entièrement fabriqués pour une construction modulaire, qui permet de bâtir entièrement la maison en un seul jour.

Una misura inusuale della proprietà con 230 m di lunghezza per 10 m di larghezza e un calcolo dei costi molto ridotto sono stati i fattori decisivi nella progettazione della "casa su trampoli". I magnifici panorami delle fattorie, dei campi e dei giardini sono stati tenuti in considerazione al momento di disegnare la pianta. Ci sono delle ampie aperture di legno nelle facciate dell'edificio in due parti, che sono rivestite con pannelli ondulati in plexiglas. Gli elementi del pavimento, delle pareti esterne e del soffitto sono completamente pronte all'uso per la costruzione modulare, consentendo di completare la costruzione della casa in un solo giorno.

GERHARD STEIXNER ARCHITEKT | VIENNA, AUSTRIA

Website	www.steixner.com
Project	art for art house
Location	Haringsee, Austria
Photos	Gerald Zugmann

The "art for art house" is unique. Because of the modular design, the façade, size, floor-plan configurations, and materials can be customized. The building offers an interior plane of 1,500 square feet, which can be flexibly arranged to allow for a number of different uses, and there is a roof-top terrace. Careful consideration was given not only to the choice of natural building materials, but also to the use of solar energy, and the building ventilation. The room climate can be adjusted by an internal sunscreen and glare shield that is supported by the built-in ventilation system, so that the temperature and air quality is kept ideal, even in summer.

Das „art for art house" ist einzigartig. Aufgrund des Moduldesigns können die Fassade, Größe, Grundrisskonfigurationen und Materialien auf die Kundenwünsche abgestimmt werden. Das Gebäude bietet eine Innenfläche von 140 m², die flexibel für eine Reihe unterschiedlicher Zwecke arrangiert werden kann, und es gibt eine Terrasse oben auf dem Dach. Es wurde nicht nur äußerste Sorgfalt auf die Auswahl natürlicher Baumaterialen verwendet, sondern auch auf die Nutzung von Solarenergie und die Belüftung des Gebäudes. Das Raumklima kann durch einen internen Sonnen- und Blendschutz geregelt werden, der durch das eingebaute Belüftungssystem unterstützt wird, so dass die Temperatur- und Luftqualität immer auf einem idealen Level gehalten wird, sogar im Sommer.

La "art for art house" (casa del arte por el arte) es única. Su diseño modular permite personalizar fachada, tamaño, plano, configuración y materiales. Esta construcción tiene una superficie de 140 m² que se pueden distribuir de forma flexible para infinidad de usos. Además, cuenta con una terraza en la azotea. Se prestó especial atención no solo a la elección de materiales de construcción naturales, sino también al uso de la energía solar y a la ventilación. La temperatura interior se ajusta mediante un filtro solar y una pantalla de protección asistida por el sistema de ventilación incorporado. La temperatura y la calidad del aire se mantienen óptimas, incluso en verano.

« La maison l'art pour l'art » (art for art house) est unique. Grâce au design modulaire, la façade, la taille, la configuration du plan d'étage et les matériaux peuvent être personnalisés. Le bâtiment offre une surface intérieure de 140 m², qui peut être aménagée de manière flexible pour permettre une variété de différents usages, et il possède un toit-terrasse. Une attention minutieuse a été apportée non seulement au choix des matériaux de construction naturels, mais aussi à l'utilisation de l'énergie solaire, et à l'aération du bâtiment. La température de la pièce peut être ajustée grâce à un écran solaire et anti-éblouissant interne dont l'action est soutenue par le système d'aération intégré, pour que la température et la qualité de l'air restent idéales, même en été.

La „art for art house" (casa di arte per arte) è unica. A causa del progetto modulare, la facciata, la misura, le configurazioni della pianta ed i materiali possono essere personalizzati. L'edificio è composto da una pianta interna di 140 m², che può essere organizzata in modo flessibile per consentire vari utilizzi e disporre inoltre di una terrazza sul tetto. E' stata data la massima attenzione non solo ai materiali di costruzione naturali, ma anche all'utilizzo di energia solare e alla ventilazione dell'edificio. Il clima della stanza può essere regolato tramite uno schermo solare interno ed uno schermo luminoso supportato dal sistema di ventilazione incorporato, così che la temperatura e la qualità dell'aria vengono mantenute a livelli ideali, anche d'estate.

SUSTAIN DESIGN STUDIO | TORONTO (ON), CANADA

Website	www.sustain.ca
Project	miniHome
Location	Toronto (ON), Canada
Building materials	Extra heavy-duty steel frame undercarriabe with triple axle assembly and detachable hitch SIPS floor structure: continuous layer of EPS insulation
Building manufacturer	Northlander Industries of Exeter
Photos	courtesy Sustain Design Studio

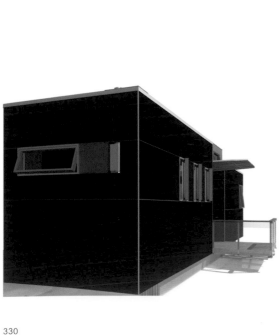

MiniHome is an elegant, modern, and yet autonomous, off-the-grid living unit with all of the comforts of home and more, built from green and sustainable materials. Different from other green and modern prefabs, it comes on wheels and can be parked anywhere—on private land or in recreational RV parks, on a lot, in a park, or on a roof. This tiny home is built green and built-to-last. It will generate no electric bill and only minimal operating costs.

Das miniHome ist eine elegante, moderne, dennoch autonome Wohneinheit jenseits des Alltäglichen mit sämtlichen Komforts eines Heimes und mehr, gebaut aus umweltfreundlichen Ökomaterialen. Im Gegensatz zu anderen „grünen" und modernen Fertighäusern kommt es auf Rädern daher und kann überall geparkt werden – auf privatem Land oder in Erholungsparks, auf einem Freigelände, in einem Park oder auf einem Dach. Dieses winzige Heim wurde nach ökologischen Gesichtspunkten gebaut und auf Langlebigkeit ausgerichtet. Dank dieser Bauweise wird es keine Stromrechnung geben, lediglich minimale Betriebskosten.

MiniHome (mini hogar) es una unidad habitacional elegante, moderna y de abastecimiento autónomo que dispone de todas las comodidades de una casa, y está construida con materiales ecológicos. A diferencia de otras casas prefabricadas ecológicas, llega sobre ruedas y se deposita en cualquier sitio: en un terreno privado, en un camping, en un solar, en un parque o sobre un tejado. Esta diminuta vivienda es ecológica y está hecha para durar. No genera facturas de electricidad y sus costes operativos son mínimos.

MiniHome est une unité de vie élégante et moderne mais cependant totalement autonome, offrant tout le confort d'un foyer et qui plus est, construite en matériaux durables et écologiques. Différente des autres préfabriqués verts modernes, elle possède des roues et peut être garée n'importe où - sur un terrain privé ou un terrain pour caravanes, sur une parcelle de terrain, dans un parc ou sur un toit. Cette minuscule maison est construite écologiquement et pour durer. Elle ne générera pas de factures d'électricité et nécessitera seulement des coûts d'opération minimes.

MiniHome è un'elegante, moderna e nonostante ciò autonoma unità abitativa non collegata alla rete comune di servizi, con tutte le comodità della casa e molto più, costruita con materiali ecologici e sostenibili. A differenza degli altri prefabbricati ecologici e moderni, si muove su ruote e può essere parcheggiata ovunque—su un terreno privato o in parchi ricreativi, in un parco o su un tetto. Questa piccola casa è costruita in modo ecologico e duraturo. Non produrrà alcuna bolletta dell'elettricità ed ha dei costi di operatività minimi.

TAYLOR SMYTH ARCHITECTS | TORONTO (ON), CANADA

Website	www.taylorsmyth.com
Project	Sunset Cabin
Location	Lake Simcoe (ON), Canada
Building materials	Structural system: wood framing on two steel beams bolted to concrete caissons.
	Exterior cladding: clear cedar screens and cedar T&G siding, green roof on 2-ply modified bitumen membrane
Building manufacturer	The Brothers Dressler/Yaan Poldaas
Photos	Ben Rahn/A-Frame Inc.

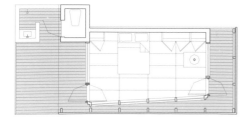

Sunset Cabin is a getaway—a separate sleeping cabin located on an existing level piece of ground, chosen both for its views and to avoid the need to remove any trees. It is supported on two steel beams resting on four concrete caissons. This allows the cabin to rest lightly on the site, with minimal disruption to the surrounding vegetation. The warm feeling of enclosure provided by the cedar screen and the interior wood surfaces of the floor, ceiling, and back wall is juxtaposed by the sensation of being at one with nature, achieved by the floor-to-ceiling glass walls on three sides.

Das Sunset Cabin ist eine Oase der Erholung. Eine separate Schlafkabine, platziert auf einem bestehenden Grundstück, das zum einen aufgrund seines Ausblicks auserwählt wurde, zum anderen, um das Fällen von Bäumen zu vermeiden. Es wird von zwei Stahlträgern gestützt, die auf vier Caissons aus Beton liegen. Dadurch liegt die Kabine nur leicht auf dem Baugelände auf und stört kaum die Vegetation rundherum. Das Gefühl der Wärme und Geborgenheit, hervorgerufen durch die Zedernholzabschirmung und die innen verarbeiteten Holzflächen des Bodens, der Decke und der Rückwand, gesellt sich zu dem Gefühl, eins mit der Natur zu sein. Dieser Effekt wird erzielt durch die auf drei Seiten befindlichen, vom Boden bis zur Decke reichenden Glaswände.

Sunset Cabin (la cabaña del atardecer) es una especie de escapada: una cabaña individual de descanso emplazada sobre un promontorio escogido por sus vistas y por no requerir la tala de árboles. Se apoya en dos vigas de acero que se asientan sobre dos cajones hidráulicos de hormigón, lo que le permite descansar sin perturbar en exceso la vegetación circundante. La cálida sensación de recogimiento que genera la pantalla de cedro y el piso interior, los techos y el tabique posterior en madera se opone a la impresión que se tiene de estar en plena naturaleza gracias a las cristaleras que van del suelo al techo en tres de los costados.

La Sunset Cabin est un refuge - une cabine de couchage séparée située sur une parcelle de terrain nivelée, choisie à la fois pour sa vue et pour éviter d'avoir à enlever des arbres. Elle est soutenue par deux poutres en acier reposant sur quatre caissons de béton. Cela permet à la cabine de reposer légèrement sur le site, en perturbant au minimum la végétation environnante. Le sentiment d'enveloppement chaleureux prodigué par l'écran de cèdre et les surfaces intérieures en bois du sol, du plafond et du mur du fond, se combine avec la sensation de ne faire qu'un avec la nature, offerte par des murs de verre du sol au plafond sur trois côtés.

La Sunset Cabin è una via di fuga—una cabina separata per dormire, situata su un livello esistente di un pezzo di terreno, scelto sia per la vista che per evitare la necessità di rimuovere qualsiasi albero. E' supportata da due pilastri di acciaio su quattro cassoni di cemento. Questo consente alla cabina di essere posata dolcemente sul sito, con un disturbo minimo per la vegetazione circostante. La sensazione calda di chiusura fornita dallo schermo in cedro e le superfici interne di legno del pavimento, del soffitto e del muro sul retro è contrapposta alla sensazione di essere un tutt'uno con la natura, raggiunta grazie alle pareti in vetro cielo-terra su tre lati.

ATELIER TEKUTO/YASUHIRO YAMASHITA | TOKYO, JAPAN

Website	www.tekuto.com
Project	aLuminum-House
Location	Kawasaki, Kanagawa Prefecture, Japan
Building materials	Prestressed aluminum structure
Photos	Makoto Yoshida

Developed for an unusually small lot, the aLuminium-House's delicate size and weight had to be carefully considered due to the site's limitations. Made from pre-stressed aluminium, the structural beam members and walls were integrated into one panel exactly 2 x 8 inches wide. As a result production costs were kept low through careful product selection and low material waste. Architecture firm Atelier Tekuto conceived of the house as an "all living" dwelling, one that would allow the homeowner's limitless choices over its function and use. To further emphasize this concept, the roof was covered with aluminium frames and honeycomb board to express a sense of infinite space.

Die besondere Größe und das Gewicht des aLuminium-House, das für ein ungewöhnlich kleines Grundstück entwickelt wurde, musste sorgfältig in Übereinstimmung mit den Beschränkungen des Grundstückes geplant werden. Gefertigt aus vorgespanntem Aluminium, wurden die Konstruktionsträgerteile in eine Platte integriert, die genau 5 x 20 cm breit ist. Daraus resultieren niedrige Produktionskosten aufgrund von sorgfältiger Produktauswahl und geringem Materialabfall. Das Architekturbüro Atelier Tekuto hat sich bei der Planung ein Haus vorgestellt, das in allen Bereichen bewohnbar ist; ein Haus, das dem Eigentümer uneingeschränkte Wahl in Bezug auf Funktion und Nutzen bietet. Um dieses Konzept zu unterstreichen, wurde das Dach mit Aluminiumrahmen und Honigwabenplatten gedeckt, so dass der Eindruck einer endlosen Geräumigkeit entsteht.

Con un tamaño y un peso muy discretos y concebida para un solar excepcionalmente pequeño, la aLuminium-House (Casa aLuminium) hay que estudiarla con detenimiento por las limitaciones de espacio. Hecha de aluminio pretensado, las vigas y la tabiquería estructural se integraron en un solo panel de 5 x 20 cm. De este modo y mediante una selección de los productos y reduciendo los residuos, se consiguieron reducir los costes de producción. El Atelier Tekuto concibió toda la casa como un espacio destinado a vivienda en el que el propietario tiene infinitas posibilidades de configurar sus funciones y usos. Para subrayarlo, se cubrió el tejado con armazones de aluminio y paneles aligerados para transmitir una sensación de espacio infinito.

L'aLuminium-House étant conçue pour une parcelle exceptionnellement petite, sa taille et son poids ont dû être soigneusement évalués en raison des limites du site. Fabriqués à base d'aluminium précontraint, les éléments des poutres et les murs de la structure sont intégrés dans un panneau mesurant exactement 5 x 20 cm de large. Les coûts de production sont donc restés bas grâce à une sélection rigoureuse des produits et à un gaspillage de matériaux réduit. Le cabinet d'architecte Atelier Tekuto a conçu la maison comme une habitation « toute vivante », qui offrirait au client un choix illimité de fonctions et d'utilisations. Pour souligner ce concept, le toit a été couvert de cadres en aluminium et d'un panneau-toiture en nid d'abeille pour exprimer un sentiment d'espace infini.

Progettata per un appezzamento di terreno inusualmente piccolo, la misura ed il peso delicati dell'aLuminium-House dovevano essere valutati con attenzione. Le parti dei pilastri e le mura strutturali in alluminio teso, sono integrate in un pannello che misura esattamente una larghezza di 5 x 20 cm. Attraverso una selezione attenta dei prodotti sono stati mantenuti bassi costi e si è ottenuto uno spreco minimo di materiale. Atelier Tekuto ha ideato la casa come una casa "tutta abitabile", una casa che permetterebbe al proprietario una scelta illimitata di funzioni e utilizzi. Per enfatizzare ulteriormente questo concetto il tetto è stato coperto con ossature di alluminio e tavole a nido d'ape che contribuiscono alla sensazione di spazio infinito.

URBAN ENVIRONMENTS ARCHITECTS, MARK MUECKENHEIM | DUSSELDORF, GERMANY

Website	www.urban-environments.net
Project	MTI - Mobile Tourist Interface
Location	Tenerife, Spain and variable
Building materials	High-tec composite shell
Renderings	urban environments architects

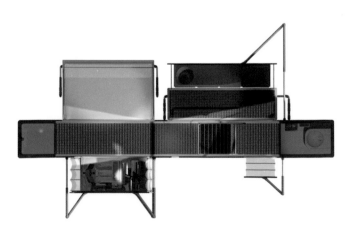

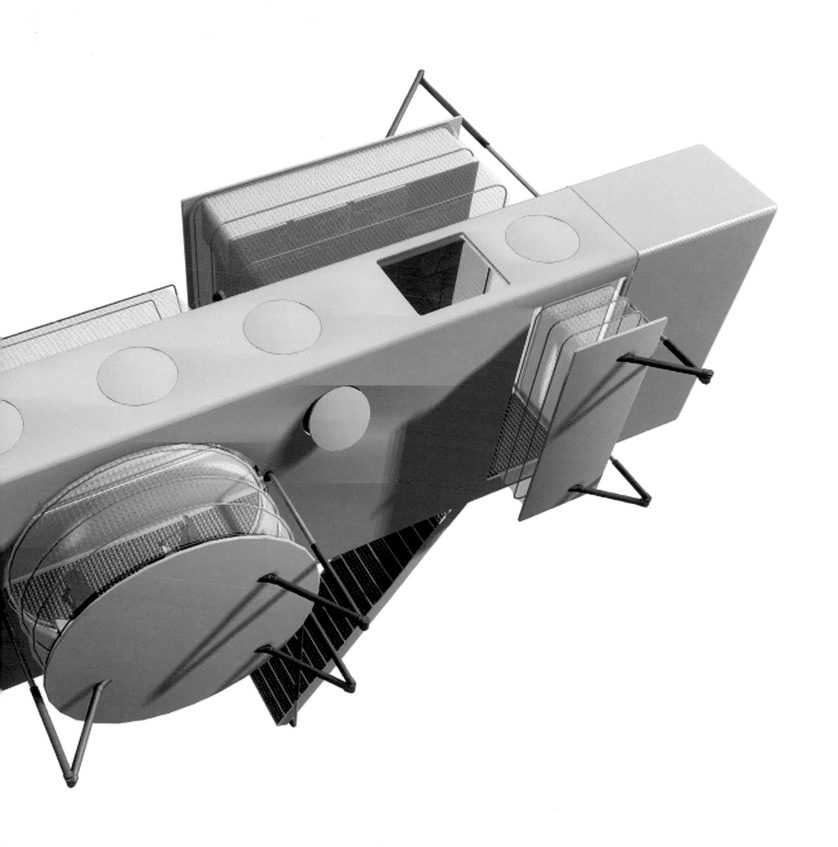

This high-tech version of the camper van started out as a project for the site-specific problems of a location in Tenerife, Spain, and later transformed into a more general unit, which could be imagined for anywhere in the world. MTI attempts to address the issue of urban sprawl in areas of tourist activity. It is a remedy against non-restricted development. Instead of building more decentralized tourist-ghettos, the units are implemented in the streetscapes of local villages. The extreme lightweight shell of the capsule, consisting of a high-tech composite material, does not require additional structural enforcement when attached to an existing building.

Diese Hightech-Version eines Wohnmobils war der Anfang eines Projektes zur Lösung der grundstückspezifischen Probleme eines Ortes auf Teneriffa, Spanien. Dieses Projekt transformierte sich später zu einer Wohneinheit für die Allgemeinheit, die man sich überall auf der Welt vorstellen kann. MTI versucht das Problem der zunehmenden Urbanisierung in Touristengegenden anzusprechen. Es geht hierbei darum, Abhilfe in Bezug auf die uneingeschränkte Entwicklung zu schaffen. Anstatt dezentralisierte Touristenghettos zu bauen, werden die Wohneinheiten in das Straßenbild der Dörfer integriert. Aufgrund der extrem leichtgewichtigen Schale der Kapsel, die aus einem Hightech-Compositmaterial besteht, ist keine zusätzliche Verstärkung der Konstruktion erforderlich, wenn sie an ein bestehendes Gebäude angefügt wird.

Esta versión high-tech de la autocaravana surgió como un proyecto específico para los problemas que planteaba un emplazamiento en Tenerife. Más tarde se transformó en una unidad más genérica y apta para cualquier parte del mundo. MTI pretende así abordar el tema de la expansión urbana en zonas turísticas. Es un remedio al desarrollismo desaforado. En lugar de crear guetos turísticos descentralizados, las unidades se instalarían en las calles de las poblaciones. La extrema ligereza del armazón de la cápsula, hecha de un compuesto de última generación, no precisa de refuerzo estructural alguno a la hora de afianzarlo a un edificio.

Cette version high-tech du camping car était au départ un projet pour résoudre les problèmes spécifiques du site de Ténérife, en Espagne, transformé ensuite pour devenir une unité plus générale, qu'on pourrait imaginer n'importe où dans le monde. Le MTI tente de résoudre le problème de l'envahissement urbain dans les zones d'activité touristique. C'est un remède au développement non-contrôlé. Au lieu de construire davantage de ghettos pour touristes décentralisés, les unités sont mises en place dans les rues des villages locaux. La coque extrêmement légère de la capsule, fabriquée dans un matériau composite high-tech, ne nécessite aucun renforcement de structure une fois attachée à un bâtiment existant.

Questa versione high-tech del camper è stata iniziata come progetto per problemi specifici legati al luogo di Tenerife, in Spagna, e più tardi è stata trasformata in un'unità più generale che poteva essere immaginata per qualsiasi posto nel mondo. MTI si propone di dare una soluzione all'espansione urbana in aree di attività turistica. E' un rimedio contro lo sviluppo incontrollato. Invece di costruire dei decentralizzati ghetti per turisti, le unità vengono implementate per le strade dei villaggi locali. L'involucro estremamente leggero della capsula, costituita da materiale composto high-tech, non richiede un rafforzamento strutturale aggiuntivo quando viene allegato all'edificio esistente.

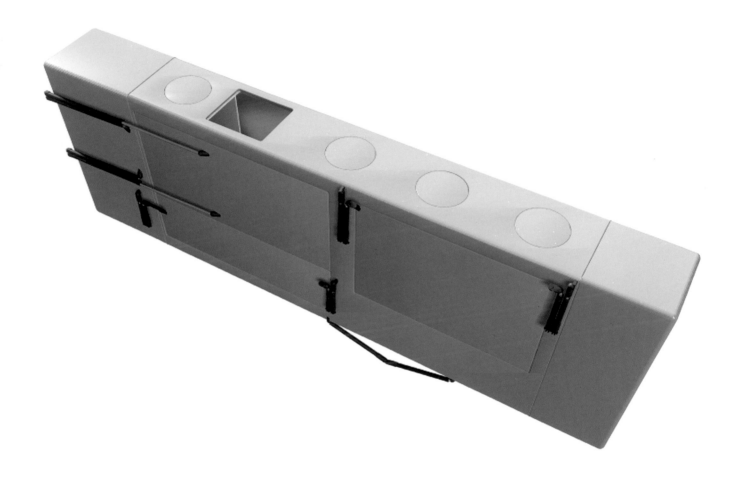

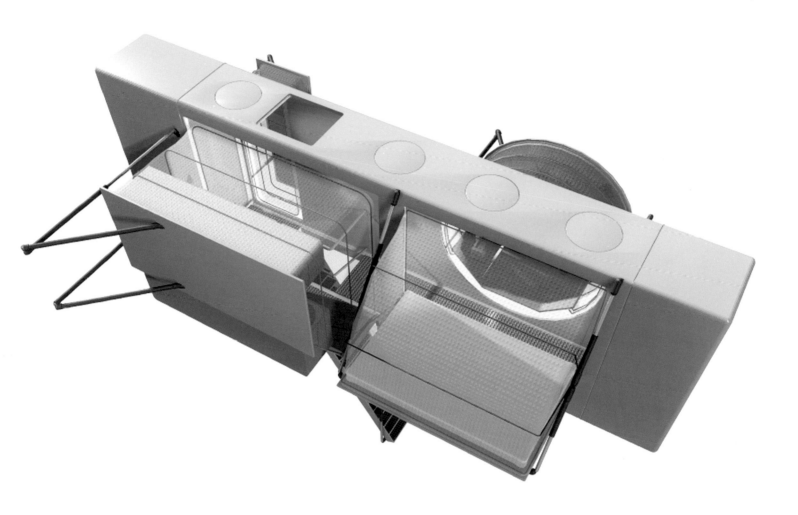

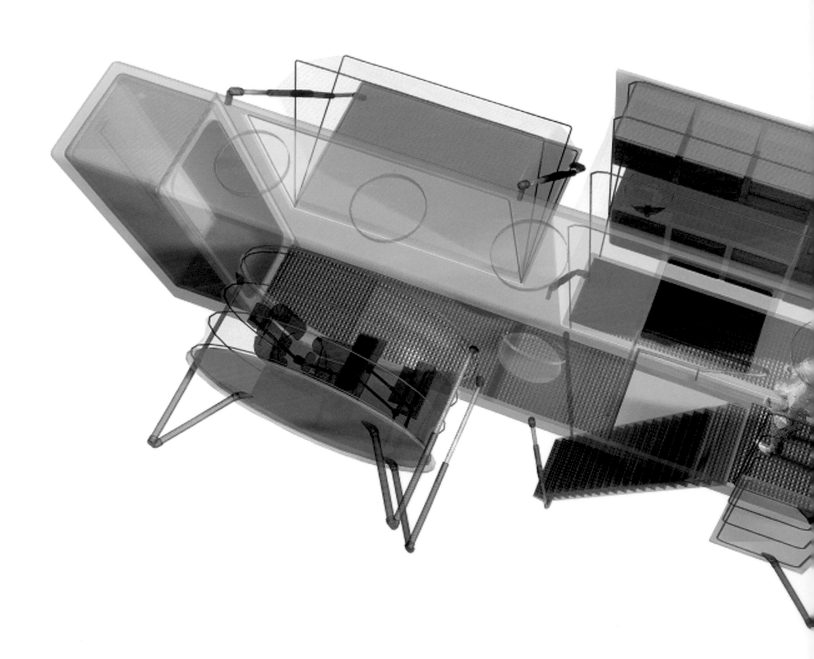

WMA WILLY MÜLLER ARCHITECTS | BARCELONA, SPAIN

Website	www.willy-muller.com
Project	House in La Floresta
Location	Sant Cugat del Vallès, Barcelona, Spain
Building materials	Steel and glass
Photos	Giovanni Zanzi

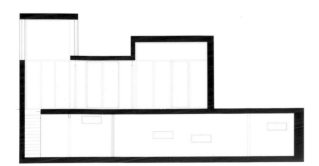

This cost-effective prototype uses innovative, off-site construction to simplify the building process without compromising the architecture of the house. The façades of the 1,615 square-foot minimalistic house are each allocated their own materiality according to their orientation. The private spaces lie in the solid base and the public spaces with terraces sit on the top level.

Dieser kostengünstige Prototyp nutzt eine innovative, außerhalb der Baustelle gefertigte Konstruktion, um den Bauprozess zu vereinfachen, ohne die Architektur des Hauses zu beeinträchtigen. Die Fassaden des 150 m² großen, minimalistischen Hauses werden jeweils mit einem individuellen Material verkleidet, das zur Orientierung dienen soll. Die Privaträume befinden sich im soliden Erdgeschoss, während die gewerblichen Räume mit den Terrassen im oberen Bereich angesiedelt sind.

Este rentable prototipo emplea un innovador sistema prefabricado de construcción que simplifica la edificación sin menoscabo de la arquitectura. Las fachadas de esta casa minimalista de 150 m² se disponen de acuerdo con su materialidad y orientación. Las áreas privadas se encuentran en la planta baja, mientras que los espacios públicos y las terrazas se sitúan en la planta superior.

Ce prototype économique utilise un système de construction hors-site innovant pour simplifier le processus sans compromettre l'architecture de la maison. Les façades de cette maison minimaliste de 150 m² ont un matériau différent selon leur orientation. Les espaces privés reposent sur la base solide et les espaces publics avec terrasses sont à l'étage.

Questo nuovo prototipo efficace dal punto di vista dei costi utilizza una costruzione innovativa lontana che esemplifica il processo di costruzione senza compromettere l'architettura della casa. Le facciate della casa minimalistica di 150 m² sono ognuna allocata secondo la propria materialità, in accordo con il proprio orientamento. Gli spazi privati si trovano sulla base solida e gli spazi pubblici con i terrazzi si trovano sul livello superiore.

ZENKAYA DESIGN/ERIC BIGOT | JOHANNESBURG, SOUTH AFRICA

Website	www.zenkaya.com
Project	Zenkaya
Location	prototype, variable
Building materials	Structural steel frame made of lip channels painted white. Insulated Structural Panel with a 75mm polystyrene panel sandwich between 2 layers of 0.5mm white Chromadek and 6mm OSB
Photos	dookphoto.com

Zenkaya's design philosophy emphasizes ultimate convenience for the client. Delivered fully constructed and ready to live in, the prefab dwelling arrives on the back of a flatbed truck. The basic Zenkaya studio module is 11 x 20 feet and features a bathroom, living and sleeping space and an optional kitchenette. The two-bedroom module is 11 x 59 feet and includes two bedrooms, a bathroom, kitchenette, living and dining space and a covered deck. Depending on the size and customization level, the unit can be developed and delivered within five to 12 weeks.

Die Designphilosophie von Zenkaya heißt optimaler Komfort für den Kunden. Vollständig konstruiert und bezugsfertig geliefert, reist die vorgefertigte Behausung auf der Ladefläche eines Pritschenwagens an. Das Zenkaya Basis Studiomodul misst 3,4 x 6 m und ist ausgestattet mit einem Badezimmer, Wohn- und Schlafraum sowie einer optionalen Kitchenette. Das Doppelbett-Schlafzimmermodul misst 3,4 x 18 m und beinhaltet zwei Schlafzimmer, ein Badezimmer, Kitchenette, Wohn- und Essbereich sowie eine überdachte Dachterrasse. Abhängig von der Größe und den Wünschen des Kunden kann die Einheit innerhalb von fünf bis 12 Wochen geplant und geliefert werden.

La filosofía del diseño de Zenkaya se centra en última instancia en las necesidades del cliente. Se entrega acabada y lista para habitar. Este hogar prefabricado se envía sobre un tráiler de suelo plano. El módulo básico de Zenkaya mide aproximadamente 3,4 x 6 m y cuenta con aseo, salón y zona de descanso, y con una minicocina opcional. El módulo de dos habitaciones mide 3,4 x 18 m e incluye dos dormitorios, aseo, minicocina, una zona se salón comedor y porche. Dependiendo del tamaño y del nivel de personalización, el plazo de entrega varía de cinco a 12 semanas.

La philosophie de design de Zenkaya met la priorité sur la commodité pour le client. Livré entièrement construit et prêt à vivre, le logement préfabriqué est livré par camion à plateforme. Le module studio Zenkaya de base mesure 3,4 x 6 m et comprend une salle de bain, un espace séjour et couchage et une kitchenette en option. Le module deux chambres mesure 3,4 x 18 m et comprend deux chambres, une salle de bain, une kitchenette, un salon-salle à manger et une terrasse couverte. Selon la taille et le niveau de personnalisation, l'unité peut être montée et livrée en cinq à douze semaines.

La filosofia del progetto di Zenkaya enfatizza la convenienza finale per il cliente. Consegnata completamente costruita e pronta per essere abitata, l'abitazione prefabbricata è trasportata sul dorso di un camion a rimorchio piano. Il modulo studio elementare Zenkaya misura 3,4 x 6,1 m e comprende un bagno, una zona soggiorno, una zona letto ed un cucinotto opzionale. Il modulo con due camere da letto misura 3,4 x 18 m ed include due camere da letto, un bagno, un cucinotto, una zona soggiorno, una zona pranzo ed uno spazio esterno coperto. A seconda della misura e del livello di personalizzazione l'unità può essere sviluppata e consegnata in cinque a 12 settimane.

INDEX

© 2007 daab
cologne   london   new york

published and distributed worldwide by
daab gmbh
friesenstr. 50
d-50670 köln

p + 49 - 221 - 913 927 0
f + 49 - 221 - 913 927 20

mail@daab-online.com
www.daab-online.com

publisher ralf daab
rdaab@daab-online.com

creative director feyyaz
mail@feyyaz.com

© 2007 edited and produced by fusion publishing gmbh stuttgart . los angeles
www.fusion-publishing.com
team michelle galindo (editor, layout), erin cullerton (introduction, texts), susan ryan (texts revisions),
jan hausberg, martin herterich (imaging & prepress), alphagriese (translation)

photo credits
coverphoto richard sprengler, backcover gerald zugmann
introduction page 9 eduardo de regules, 11 sascha kletsch, 13 makoto yoshida

printed in china
www.everbest.eu

isbn 978-3-86654-022-4